Making Sense of Number, K-10

Getting to know your students so you can support the development
of their mathematical understanding

Mary Fiore

Ryan Tackaberry

Pembroke Publishers Limited

© 2018 Pembroke Publishers
538 Hood Road
Markham, Ontario, Canada L3R 3K9
www.pembrokepublishers.com

Distributed in the U.S. by Stenhouse Publishers
www.stenhouse.com

Funded by the Government of Canada
Financé par le gouvernement du Canada | Canada

Library and Archives Canada Cataloguing in Publication

Fiore, Mary, author
    Making sense of number : getting to know your students so you can support the
development of their mathematical understanding / Mary Fiore, Ryan Tackaberry.

Includes index.
Issued in print and electronic formats.
ISBN 978-1-55138-332-3 (softcover).--ISBN 978-1-55138-933-2 (PDF)

    1. Mathematics--Study and teaching. 2. Teacher-student relationships. I. Tackaberry,
Ryan, author II. Title.

QA11.2.F56 2018   510.71   C2018-903295-2
                                        C2018-903296-0

Editor: Janice Dyer
Cover Design: John Zehethofer
Typesetting: Jay Tee Graphics Ltd.

Printed and bound in Canada
9 8 7 6 5 4 3 2 1

Contents

Acknowledgments

From Mary Fiore:

I have always been inspired by the phrase "create the life you want to live," but I would not have been able to do so without my various pillars of strength. Mena, this dedication is for you, for all your strength, love, and support over the years.

And to my dear friend and co-author: Ryan, together we have made sense of number, but I thank you for helping me make sense of friendship.

From Ryan Tackaberry:

For the little sweet things in my life—you are why I do this work.

And to Mary, my co-author: You are a friend far above the mean and median of friends. Not your average MF. Thank you.

From both of us:

This book is the result of our professional wonderings and extends beyond the two of us. We are most grateful to our students, parents, and colleagues for supporting our learning as we move along our professional learning journeys focusing on the teaching and learning of mathematics.

To Mary Macchiusi: Thank you for supporting our vision and providing us with an opportunity to represent our thinking.

To Janice Dyer: Thank you for your efforts as an editor and for clearly representing our thoughts and ideas. Your wonderings contributed to our on-going reflections and your suggestions supported the synthesis of our thinking.

Preface

Supporting Reflective Learning

In developing this professional learning support, our goal was to provide educators with an opportunity to reflect on their thinking and the thinking of their students. *Reflection* is integral to both teaching and learning. Teachers reflect when they:
- plan for meaningful experiences to elicit student thinking and promote learning with understanding;
- consider student learning needs to set goals; and
- address their professional learning needs as part of their own ongoing teacher growth.

Students reflect when they:
- monitor their thought processes and learning;
- think about how to expand their understanding by transferring learning to new contexts;
- make connections between their thinking and the thinking of others; and
- make connections between mathematical concepts.

Through reflecting, we make connections between our thinking and our students' thinking so we can better know them and plan for meaningful learning experiences that enhance their mathematical thinking and understanding. When we know our learners, being responsive becomes less intrusive and more fluid. Knowing our learners helps us to know ourselves as learners of mathematics so that collectively, with our students, we can *make sense of number*.

This book is a product of our reflection and a synthesis of our thinking about teaching and learning mathematics. We invite readers to engage with the material presented in this book as part of their reflective practice and ongoing professional learning.

Making Sense of Reflection

As educators, our knowledge and understanding of teaching and learning develops by reflecting on a series of questions as we move along our professional learning journey:

- What affirms my thinking?
- What challenges and extends my thinking?
- How can I build upon my students' thinking?
- What do I need to learn to support their learning?
- How will I implement what I have learned?
- How will I know they have learned it?

Without a clear understanding of what it means to reflect, professional learning in an attempt to support student learning becomes a daunting task. As Dewey states, "We do not learn from experience … we learn from reflecting on experience."

As educators with a passionate commitment to the teaching and learning of mathematics, we are particularly drawn to Dewey's description of reflection, which states that reflection involves a consecutive ordering:

> "Reflection involves not simply a sequence of ideas, but a *con*sequence—a consecutive ordering is such a way that each determines the next as its proper outcome, while each in turn leans back on its predecessors. The successive portions of the reflective thought grow out of one another and support one another; they do not come and go in a medley. Each phase is a step from something to something—technically speaking, it is a term of thought. Each term leaves a deposit which is utilized in the next term." (Dewey, 1933, p. 6)

This description implies thinking differently about things and doing things differently based on a new understanding—a new learning. This parallels planning for a consecutive ordering of meaningful learning experiences based on what we know about our mathematical learners and where we want our mathematical learners to be along a learning progression. The learning experiences embedded throughout this book follow a consecutive ordering based on our understanding of learning progressions to support making sense of key number concepts.

The five steps of reflection, as noted by Dewey (1933), include:
1. identifying a difficulty;
2. developing a deeper understanding of the difficulty;
3. developing a possible solution;
4. subjecting the possible solution to scrutiny and reasoning; and
5. putting the solution into practice and gathering evidence of impact.

The following image represents professional learning as a cyclical, reflective process.

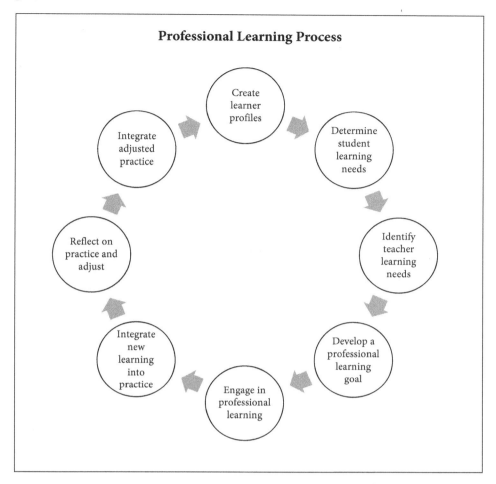

(Fiore & Lebar, 2017)

Opportunity for Reflection

What are the connections between the five steps of reflection as identified by Dewey and the professional learning process?

Reading and Using this Book

Knowing Your Learner is designed for educators—teachers, administrators, and other instructional leaders—who share an instructional focus on knowing and responding to learners in the classroom. It serves as a guide to understanding where a learner is developmentally and provides a framework to support individual learning needs with rich learning experiences. It is our intention to support conversations about how important math concepts can emerge throughout each of the strands in mathematics.

To support ongoing professional learning, we have embedded opportunities to engage in reflective thought throughout this book. The *Opportunity for Reflection* boxes are designed to prompt reflection as part of planning for meaningful learning experiences with the goal of eliciting student thinking and promoting an understanding of number. While engaging with the material presented in this book, we encourage readers to reflect on how to modify and use some of the questions posed. For example, we use a Frayer Model in Chapter 2 to represent our synthesized thinking of mathematical proficiency. How might you use this model with students to synthesize their understanding of a mathematical concept?

Prompting Further Reflection

In addition to the *Opportunity for Reflection* boxes embedded throughout the book, we have incorporated other components to prompt continuous reflection:

- *Vignettes*: The vignettes at the beginning of each chapter are designed to invite you to make connections to your experience as learners of mathematics at various stages of your mathematical journey (i.e., learners of mathematics as students and as teachers).
- *The Important Stuff*: Throughout Chapters 3–6, we have elaborated on key number concepts in boxes labelled *The Important Stuff*. Big ideas are statements that link mathematical concepts between various strands into a coherent whole; bigger ideas are statements that describe the mental actions or processes associated with various thinking skills. We provide innovative variations on those statements by proposing that in addition to considering the big ideas and the bigger ideas, readers also consider the *important stuff*: statements that describe key number concepts to support number sense.
- *Sample Progressions:* We have synthesized our understanding of learning progressions and have provided examples of progressions of student learning for each of the key number concepts. We encourage you to make connections between these progressions, other progressions you may have used, and the mathematics curriculum as you plan for learning experiences.
- *Planning to Meet Your Learner*: We have developed learning experiences designed to promote understanding of key number concepts by connecting number sense to other strands in math. The learning experiences align with how students learn mathematics developmentally.

Featured Learning Experiences

The learning experiences provided in Chapters 3–6, across three school divisions, are designed to meet learners along their mathematical journey. Each learning experience includes:

- an outline of the *important stuff* associated with each of the key number concepts;
- a description of the key number concepts along a sample learning progression;
- thinking stems and prompting questions to support the development of the key number concepts;
- learning experiences focused on each of the key number concepts, along with possible learning intentions, success criteria, what teachers may know about

their learner, and what teachers want their learner to know; these learning experiences are designed to develop students' conceptual understanding of key number concepts and highlight specific student thinking (i.e., what the student might be saying and doing and how they might represent their thinking) and teacher thinking (i.e., what the teacher is noticing, how they might interpret what they are noticing, how they might confirm their thinking, and how they might respond); and

- opportunities for reflection to enhance professional learning.

The focus on key number concepts provides opportunities to explore the mathematics curriculum through the *important stuff* to enhance students' understanding of mathematical concepts and skills. *Making Sense of Number* is an opportunity for us to reflect on how the use of learning progressions helps us to plan for learning experiences by better understanding our learners' thinking. By noticing, interpreting, confirming, and responding to student thinking, we can better understand our students and develop their mathematical understanding.

A Vision for Teaching and Learning Mathematics

Imagine learning spaces where teachers believe they can influence student learning and elicit and develop mathematical thinking, and students believe in their abilities as young mathematical thinkers and learners. Teachers share learning intentions and criteria with students, and students have an opportunity to clarify their understanding of the learning intentions so they can reflect on and monitor their own learning. Teachers purposefully plan meaningful learning experiences, which address where students are along their mathematical learning journey and build upon students' lives, interests, strengths, and needs. Students reflect on which strategies and thinking tools they are going to use to communicate their mathematical thinking as they work to make sense of mathematical concepts and skills. As students engage with the mathematical task, teachers pose questions to elicit further thinking and promote a deep understanding. Students make their mathematical thinking visible and identify connections between their thinking and the thinking of others, asking each other questions to enhance their learning. Teachers notice, interpret, and confirm students' mathematical thinking and respond to what is being noticed. Teachers and students share a common belief about the teaching and learning of mathematics and what constitutes mathematics.

The learning space described above reflects a vision for teaching and learning mathematics where the focus is on learning as a process rather than as a product. As implied in this description, the teaching and learning of mathematics consists of many interconnected parts. A sound mathematics and learning vision helps teachers draw upon and use their understanding of pedagogy, curricula, and their learners to plan for meaningful learning experiences. To clarify our vision for effective mathematics teaching and learning, it is important to establish a common understanding of what we mean by each component: teaching, learning, and mathematics.

Opportunity for Reflection

How would you describe teaching and learning? How would you describe the teaching and learning of mathematics?

Beliefs about Mathematics

There are varying perspectives on what constitutes mathematics in educational settings. Some describe mathematics as looking for and recognizing patterns, while others view mathematics as a set of algorithms or procedures that need to be followed. A vision for teaching and learning mathematics that reflects the learning space described in the opening vignette includes a belief that mathematics is a way of *thinking* about things. Such a belief lends itself to practices where the focus is on eliciting mathematical thinking to make sense of mathematics concepts and skills. Our practice and beliefs about mathematics are related to the teaching and learning of mathematics (Beswick, 2005). If we believe, for example, that mathematics is about numbers, rules, and algebra, our practice may reflect that belief, such as only exposing students to a standard algorithm when teaching the multiplication of two-digit numbers. If, on the other hand, we view mathematics as a way of thinking about things, we may present students with various models and provide opportunities to make connections between the models to support understanding.

Parents' attitudes and beliefs about mathematics may also influence their views about their children's mathematical learning experiences. For example, if a parent or caregiver believes that mathematics is about numbers and the use of formulas and rules, they may expect their children to engage with learning experiences that promote the use of rules, formulas, or a series of steps. In addition, parents might need opportunities to make sense of mathematical experiences that promote mathematical thinking and sense making. For instance, they might need opportunities to make sense of how mathematical questions such as "The perimeter is 50, what might the length and width be?" enhance the learning experience and provide opportunities for students to develop a deep understanding so they can transfer this learning and understanding to new contexts. (We will further explore different types of learning later in this chapter.)

Parallel to this view are the students' attitudes and beliefs about mathematics. For example, if students view mathematics as only operations with numbers, they might operate on the numbers without reflecting on the reasonableness of their solutions; they do not view math as a way of thinking about things. It is important to clarify that learning experiences such as these *can* elicit mathematical thinking and enhance students' understanding of mathematical concepts and skills. The learning experiences, along with the learning space and what happens within the learning space (e.g., learner/learner interactions, teacher/learner interactions) are what constitute meaningful learning experiences. The learning experience is enhanced by asking a question such as, "I noticed you used a formula as part of your solution. How else might you show your thinking?" or by having students share their thinking with each other with an emphasis on justifying and defending ideas.

Teaching and Learning Mathematics

When we have a deep understanding of teaching and learning, we are able to provide high-quality mathematics instruction for all students. *Teaching* refers to everything we do to support student learning, including knowing about students, pedagogy, and subject-specific content knowledge unique to teaching. Teaching includes instructional practices and other components (Beck & Kosnik, 2014), such as:

- helping students understand the world;
- helping students develop a viable way of life;
- building a safe and inclusive class community; and
- establishing a strong teacher–student relationship.

Teaching also includes effective assessment practices, such as attending to particular events in an instructional setting, interpreting events in an instructional setting, building an understanding of student thinking and learning, and deciding how to respond on the basis of student understanding (Jacobs et al., 2011).

Although there are varying descriptions of what constitutes *learning*, the notion of experiencing permanent changes in the way we think and how we do things remains consistent. In other words, learning involves moving beyond existing routines and requires people to rethink ideas, practices, and attitudes and values to change what they are doing (Hammerness et al., 2008). The shift in thinking and behavior, regardless of whether we are focusing on teacher learning or student learning, indicates a deep learning that is transferrable to other contexts. The most important part of this description of learning is "permanent change." For example, consider a student who, at an early age, memorized one of the standard algorithms for the multiplication of two-digit numbers and has relied on this standard algorithm into adulthood (see Figure 1.1). This individual relies on the steps without understanding why "carrying was used" or why a "zero was used as a placeholder"; they simply memorized the procedure.

Steps:
1. Multiply 8 × 67:
   - 8 × 7 = 56 Write down 6 and carry the 5.
   - 8 × 6 = 48 Add 5 to 48 and write down 53.
2. Cross out the carried 5.
3. Write a 0 beneath the 6 as a placeholder.
4. Multiply 4 × 67:
   - 4 × 7 = 28 Write down the 8 and carry the 2.
   - 4 × 6 = 24 Add 2 to 24 and write down 26.
5. Add the ones, tens, hundreds, and thousands.

$$
\begin{array}{r}
2\,\not{5} \\
67 \\
\times\quad 48 \\
\hline
536 \\
2680 \\
\hline
3216
\end{array}
$$

Figure 1.1: Multiplication Using the Standard Algorithm

Opportunity for Reflection

Based on your thinking about and understanding of learning, does this student's experience in the early grades constitute learning?

Now consider another student who, early in their learning journey, relied on the same standard algorithm, but then was provided with an opportunity to make sense of various strategies that could be used to multiply two-digit numbers (see Figure 1.2). The student not only made sense of the various strategies, but also was able to make connections between the standard algorithm and the various models. Despite understanding many strategies using different models to support understanding, the student relies especially on breaking multiplicative situations into parts using an area model to visually show the situation. This individual continues to rely on this model as an adult when faced with the task of multiplying without the use of a tool.

Steps:
1. Draw a rectangle. Divide the rectangle into four boxes.
2. Break the numbers being multiplied into tens and ones. Write the tens and ones for the first number along the top of the grid, and for the second number along the side of the grid.
3. Multiply each rectangle: 30 × 20 = 600; 30 × 8 = 240; 4 × 20 =80; 4 × 8 = 32
4. Add all the numbers in the rectangle.

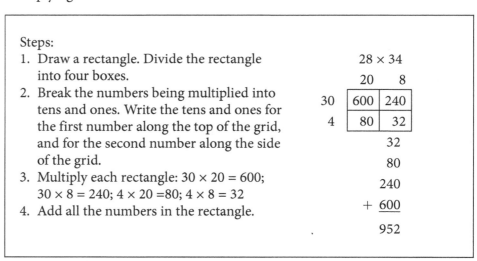

Figure 1.2: Multiplication Using an Area Model

"Professional learning can have a powerful effect on teacher skills and knowledge and on student learning if it is sustained over time, focused on important content, and embedded in the work of professional learning communities that support ongoing improvements in teachers' practice. When well-designed, these opportunities help teachers master content, hone teaching skills, evaluate their own and their students' performance, and address changes needed in teaching and learning in their schools."
Darling-Hammond et al., 2009, p. 7

The notion of learning as "a permanent change" applies to educators as well. Most of us can recall an experience in which we listened to and participated in a presentation, but where we may not have been able to make connections to the ideas being presented. We may have enjoyed the energy of the presenter and the content, but the opportunity may not have enabled us to change the way we think about things or do things. In other words, nothing we did changed following this opportunity. Katz and Dack (2013) call this type of experience "professional development" rather than "professional learning." Most of us can also probably recall a professional learning opportunity where we felt inspired, motivated, and eager to apply the new learning with our students. This learning changed the way we introduced the particular topic or idea to our students.

Opportunity for Reflection

Think of a professional learning opportunity that you participated in that resulted in a permanent shift in the way you thought about an idea. How did this permanent shift in thinking affect what you did in the classroom?

Throughout this book, we will be exploring the various facets of teaching and learning to enhance mathematical learning experiences for both teachers and students. It is difficult—in fact, almost impossible—to separate teaching from learning; our intention is to purposefully consider them as inseparable identities. Learning happens within meaningful experiences where the educator is guiding and participating in the learning—*teaching*. It is just as difficult to separate teacher learning from student learning. Consider the learning experience presented in Figure 1.2 on the previous page that resulted in a permanent shift in the way the student approached the multiplication of two-digit numbers. There is a very good chance that the teacher of that student, at some point, engaged in professional learning to learn something new about multiplication so their students would understand multiplication differently.

"Simply knowing the areas in which students are struggling is not enough for teachers to be able to teach differently. So what comes next? It is important to understand that teachers teach what they know about a concept. Changing teaching means changing the understanding that underlies the teaching."
Katz & Dack, 2013, p. 5

Knowledge to Support the Teaching and Learning of Mathematics

Teachers need to have different types of knowledge to support the teaching and learning of mathematics. Although, first and foremost, we need to have knowledge of our learners, we also need to have knowledge of effective instructional practices that influence student learning, commonly referred to as pedagogical knowledge (Schulman, 1987). These types of knowledge are cross-curricular in nature and are not specific to the teaching and learning of mathematics. However, since our focus is on the teaching and learning of mathematics, there is another specific type of knowledge required, which is often referred to as *knowing mathematics for teaching* or *mathematical knowledge for teaching* (Ball et al., 2005). As part of our vision for teaching and learning mathematics, it is important for us to bridge the various types of knowledge to effectively support a range of learners.

Knowing Mathematics for Teaching

Mathematical knowledge for teaching includes, for example, having knowledge of:
- what constitutes additive thinking and multiplicative thinking;
- how students learn mathematics developmentally (e.g., progressing from additive thinking to multiplicative thinking);
- possible errors and misconceptions and reasons why these errors and misconceptions might occur; and
- strategies and models that help students shift their thinking from additive thinking to multiplicative thinking.

Specifically, teachers who know mathematics for teaching have knowledge of or the ability to do the following:
- Understand student development when learning mathematics.
- Use and choose strategies and models to enhance thinking and learning.
- Build students' trust and self-efficacy.
- Pose meaningful mathematical questions.
- Give and appraise explanations.
- Select or design tasks.
- Use and choose multiple representations.
- Note students' mathematical thinking.
- Analyze student errors.
- Address possible misconceptions.
- Facilitate mathematical discourse.
- Define terms mathematically.
- Know when a student's answer is incorrect (i.e., mathematically, what could have been done wrong), know why a student might have made the error, and have the mathematical understanding needed to respond to the student.
- Demonstrate how to carry out a procedure or algorithm.
- Use appropriate mathematical language.

(Adapted from Thames & Ball, 2010)

Opportunity for Reflection

What mathematical knowledge for teaching would you need to have to respond to the following student response? As part of your reflection, consider the following questions:
- What do you think the student did wrong mathematically?
- Why do you think the student did this?
- What mathematical understanding would you need to have to respond to the student?

Jonathan has 24 m of fencing. He wants to build a closed-in area for his new puppy. How much area might the puppy have to run around?

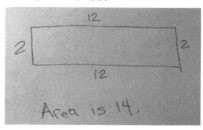

Knowing Your Mathematical Learner

"Knowing mathematics for teaching demands a kind of depth and detail that goes well beyond what is needed to carry out the algorithm reliably." *Ball et al., p. 22*

While we need to have knowledge of pedagogy to support the teaching and learning of mathematics, only when we understand our learners can we apply our knowledge and understanding of effective pedagogical practices in meaningful ways. The purpose of meaningful learning experiences is student learning; the intended outcome of this learning experience is for students to have a deep conceptual understanding of mathematics concepts and skills and number sense. It is important to consider learning as a process and not as an outcome or product.

To better understand learners, the Ontario Ministry of Education (2013) suggests that teachers develop student profiles. Student profiles provide information about the learning strengths and needs of individual students and act as a tool for planning precise and personalized assessment and instruction. Appendix A provides a sample student profile template.

Why Develop a Student Profile?

Developing an individual student profile allows us to:
- consider how to use and build on the student's strengths;
- consider ways of motivating the student and supporting their learning in a particular subject by drawing on strengths that the student has demonstrated in other subjects, prior knowledge in various subjects, learning style or preference, and interests outside school;
- develop specifically targeted assessment and instruction for the student;
- consider how the student would benefit from particular groupings of students for different kinds of activities; and
- foresee the need for, and plan for the use of, supports and accommodations, appropriate media and technologies, and particular forms and modes of instructional and assessment activities, tools, and resources.

(Ontario Ministry of Education, 2013)

Planning for Meaningful Learning

Once we have mathematical knowledge for teaching and knowledge of our mathematical learners, we are ready to plan meaningful learning experiences. Specifically, consider the steps for planning a meaningful learning environment: The process of planning for learning includes ensuring the outcome is a meaningful learning experience, and the outcome of the learning experience is number sense and a conceptual understanding of mathematics concepts and skills.

There are various outcomes in the teaching and learning process (see Figure 1.3).

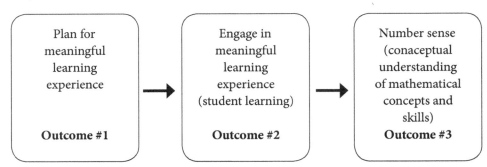

Figure 1.3: Teaching and Learning Outcomes

"Since all students are capable and bring a wide range of experiential, cultural, and linguistic resources to the classroom, our job as teachers is to figure out ways to regularly use these resources and to give them a place of prominence in what counts in the classroom." *Lewison et al., 2008, p. 28*

Recognizing that the backward design process, or beginning with the end in mind, is a suggested planning sequence for meaningful learning environments where the desired result is student learning (outcome #2), we decided to begin with the learner (Wiggins & McTighe, 1998). Recognizing what students should know, understand, and be able to do is a necessary part of the planning process, as is knowing our learners. Without a deep understanding of who our learners are (i.e., their strengths, needs, and learning preferences), planning for learning becomes challenging to differentiate. We can only differentiate instruction and assessment when we know our mathematical learners. Placing our learners at the front of the planning process as personal and cultural resources will help us plan for learning (see Figure 1.4).

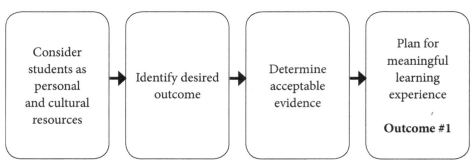

Figure 1.4: Steps before Outcome #1

When planning for meaningful learning experiences, it is useful to think of the different categories of learning: surface, deep, and transfer. We have adopted these three phases of learning as part of our desired outcome when planning for meaningful learning (see Figure 1.5). It is important to note that the proposed phases of learning are not intended to be linear; instead, learning will be different based on students' strengths, needs, and interests.

PHASES OF LEARNING

Learning	What Happens	What Doesn't Happen Yet
Surface Learning	• Introduce new ideas • Develop conceptual understanding • Develop procedural fluency	• Make connections between conceptual understandings about one topic to another topic • Apply understanding to more complex real-world situations
Deep Learning	• Plan, investigate, and elaborate on conceptual understanding • Make generalizations • Make decisions about which tools and strategies to use • Consolidate understanding of mathematical concepts and procedures • Make deeper connections between ideas • Use efficient and flexible ways of thinking about concepts	• Identify similarities and differences between concepts • Make connections between a previously learned task and a novel situation • Self-moderate • Self-direct
Transfer Learning	• Apply knowledge, skills, and strategies to new tasks and new situations • Think metacognitively • Self-monitor learning • Recognize how mathematics is used to make sense of the world • Desire to solve new and complex problems on their own	

Figure 1.5

(Adapted from Hattie, Fisher, & Frey, 2017)

"Note that surface learning does not mean superficial learning. Rather, surface learning is a time when students initially are exposed to concepts, skills, and strategies. Surface learning is critical, because it provides a foundation on which to build as students are asked to think more deeply." *Hattie et al., p. 9*

Consider the following measurement example: The area of a circle is denoted by πr^2.

- *Surface knowledge* focuses on students understanding that r represents the radius of a circle and that π represents *Pi* and has a value of approximately 3.14.
- *Deep learning* requires students to understand and show that π is derived from knowing the circumference and diameter of a circle and understanding the relationship between diameter and radius.
- *Transfer learning* requires students to apply their knowledge and understanding to situations requiring them to solve problems involving the estimation and calculation of a circle.

Using Learning Progressions

Much of the recent research on the teaching and learning of mathematics incorporates the use of learning progressions, also called learning trajectories, to help teachers plan for a combination of surface, deep, and transfer learning (see Clements & Sarama, 2014, for examples of learning progressions). Learning progressions help us meet our students where they are and build on what they know. Mathematical learning progressions help us to better understand our mathematical learners by providing us with the opportunity to make sense of how mathematical concepts and skills develop over time. According to Clements and Sarama (2014), learning trajectories have three parts:

1. a specific mathematical goal;
2. a path along which students develop to reach that goal; and
3. a set of instructional activities that help students move along that path.

Some learning progressions model student learning about mathematical concepts, such as fractions or measurement (Simon & Tzur, 2004; Szilagyi, et al., 2013; Small, 2005); others serve as a tool for teachers to use to think about their instruction (Sztajn et al., 2012). Although there are varying interpretations and applications of learning progressions, they all share a common purpose: they help us to better understand how students learn mathematics developmentally and help us plan for meaning learning experiences (see Outcome #1 in Figure 1.3).

Opportunity for Reflection

What mathematical knowledge for teaching would you need to respond to the following student responses to the mathematical question presented? How might you respond in the moment to each learner to nudge them along a learning progression?

 How many pieces fill a game board?

Student 1: Counts by ones starting in the bottom left corner.
Student 2: Counts by twos.
Student 3: Multiplies 5×7 then adds 7 more.

Student 1   Student 2   Student 3

Professional Noticing

We have addressed the different types of knowledge teachers need to plan for meaningful learning to promote surface, deep, and transfer learning. Ultimately, our vision for teaching and learning mathematics includes students being able to transfer their knowledge and understanding to new contexts as they engage in reflective thought about their learning. We want them to be able to intuitively think mathematically so they can embrace mathematics as a way of thinking about things. This then begs the question: How will we know our students are engaging in thinking and learning?

Consider outcome #2 in Figure 1.3, *engage in meaningful learning experience*, where the outcome is student learning. If we want to engage students in learning and we believe that learning happens as students engage in mathematical thinking, how do we ensure that mathematical thinking is happening? This brings us to the notion of professional noticing (Jacobs et al., 2010; Mason, 2000). Learning progressions support professional noticing by helping us to clarify what it is we are trying to attend to or *notice*, which is thinking, learning, and eventually number sense. Learning progressions help us to identify what it is we are looking for and what we see, and they help us to make sense of what we see (Sherin et al., 2011).

Our definition of professional noticing includes the following:

- attending to students' strategies;
- interpreting students' thinking and understanding;
- confirming interpretations; and
- deciding how to respond on the basis of the confirmed interpretation of students' understanding.

(Adapted from Jacobs et al., 2010)

We engage in professional noticing when we attend to our students' thinking (noticing), interpret our students' thinking, confirm our thinking about our students' thinking and understanding, and decide how to respond so that students can made sense of mathematical concepts and skills. We can use professional noticing to indicate the act of observing or recognizing something as we engage in meaningful learning experiences (Sherin et al., 2011). Eliciting and noticing student thinking and understanding is integral to meaningful mathematical learning experiences. By noticing, interpreting, confirming, and deciding how to respond to student thinking, we are promoting mathematical thinking and number sense. The learning experiences presented in Chapters 3–6 specifically address what teachers attend to as students engage with mathematical learning experiences, purposefully developed to support mathematical thinking and number sense across various mathematical strands.

Teaching and Learning for Mathematical Proficiency

As our vision for effective mathematics teaching and learning evolves over time, we look to gain an understanding of how numerate students interact with the world around them. The National Research Council (2001) states that the teaching and learning of mathematics includes the development of five inter-related strands that, collectively, constitute mathematical proficiency: conceptual understanding; procedural fluency; strategic competence; adaptive reasoning; and productive disposition. Teaching and learning for mathematical proficiency incorporates teaching for mathematical thinking.

"So, teachers who understand learning trajectories understand the math, the way children think and learn about math, and how to help children learn it better." *Clements & Sarama, 2014, p. ix*

"If we want to support students in learning, and we believe that learning is a product of thinking, then we need to be clear about what it is we are trying to support." *Ritchhart et al., 2011, p. 5*

"Hearing the mathematics in a child's idea is a basic task of noticing in teaching." *Ball, 2011, p. xxiii*

The Components of Mathematical Proficiency

The following graphic organizers, or Frayer models, adapted from the National Research Council (2001), synthesize our understanding of the various components of mathematical proficiency.

Note: The solution for "What it isn't" represents one example of student thinking. On its own, it does not necessarily represent a conceptual understanding. Rather, it demonstrates the use of an algorithm. We would have to gather other evidence of student thinking and understanding (e.g., something we noticed or something we heard while engaging in a conversation with the student).

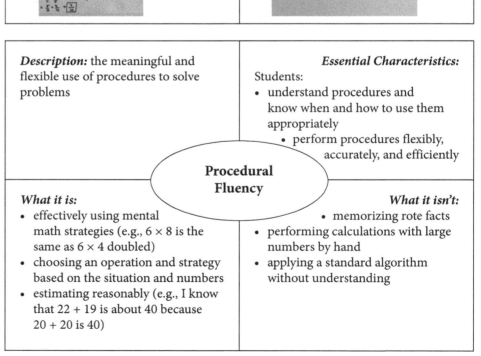

Description: the comprehension and connection of concepts, operations, and relations

Essential Characteristics:
Students:
- understand the importance of a mathematical idea and in which contexts it is useful
- learn facts and methods and/or procedures
- organize their knowledge into a coherent whole
- represent mathematical ideas in different ways and know how different representations can be useful for different purposes

Conceptual Understanding

What it is:
- Find the sum of $\frac{1}{2} + \frac{2}{5}$.

What it isn't:
- Find the sum of $\frac{1}{2} + \frac{2}{5}$.

Description: the meaningful and flexible use of procedures to solve problems

Essential Characteristics:
Students:
- understand procedures and know when and how to use them appropriately
- perform procedures flexibly, accurately, and efficiently

Procedural Fluency

What it is:
- effectively using mental math strategies (e.g., 6×8 is the same as 6×4 doubled)
- choosing an operation and strategy based on the situation and numbers
- estimating reasonably (e.g., I know that $22 + 19$ is about 40 because $20 + 20$ is 40)

What it isn't:
- memorizing rote facts
- performing calculations with large numbers by hand
- applying a standard algorithm without understanding

Description: the ability to formulate, represent, and solve mathematical problems

Essential Characteristics:

Students:

- generate a mathematical representation of the problem and ignore irrelevant features
- identify the mathematics they need to solve the problem
- understand various strategies and models

Strategic Competence

What it is:

- representing a problem accurately
- identifying key features to ensure the problem is understood

Jonathan ordered a pizza with 18 slices. The next day $\frac{2}{3}$ of the pizza remained. Jonathan then eats $\frac{1}{2}$ of what remains. How many pieces did he eat?

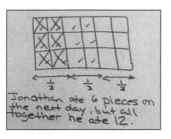

Jonathan ate 6 pieces on the next day, but all together he ate 12.

What it isn't:

- "number grabbing" (e.g., selecting numbers and performing operations)
- relying on a previous experience that used an algorithm and performing what is recalled and memorized

Jonathan ordered a pizza with 18 slices. The next day $\frac{2}{3}$ of the pizza remained. Jonathan then eats $\frac{1}{2}$ of what remains. How many pieces did he eat?

$$\frac{2}{3} \text{ of } 18$$

$$\frac{2}{3} \times \cancel{18}^{6} = 12$$

$$\frac{1}{2} \text{ of } 12$$

$$\frac{1}{2} \times \cancel{12}^{6} = 6$$

Description: the capacity to think logically about the relationships among concepts and situations

Essential Characteristics:
Students:
- justify conclusions
- make sense of mathematical facts, procedures, concepts, and strategies and/or methods
- monitor their own progress and generate alternative plans if the current plan is ineffective

Adaptive Reasoning

What it is:
- inductive reasoning (e.g., identify patterns by considering multiple instances)
- intuitive reasoning
- making inferences (e.g., student draws meaning from explicit and implicit information using prior knowledge and experiences)
- reasoning and proving mathematical thinking

What it isn't:
- justifying procedures only once (e.g., it isn't adaptive reasoning if students can only practise problems on multiplying fractions after the procedure has been introduced)

Description: the tendency to see sense in mathematics, to perceive it as both useful and worthwhile

Essential Characteristics:
Students:
- believe that steady effort in learning mathematics pays off
- see themselves as effective learners and doers of mathematics

Productive Disposition

What it is:
- viewing mathematics as understandable and not arbitrary
- displaying positive attitudes and beliefs about yourself as a mathematics learner

What it isn't:
- relying on memorizing rather than sense-making to solve problems
- viewing mathematical ability as fixed (e.g., not everyone can do math)
- viewing test questions and results of tests as the only measures of ability

Structuring Learning Experiences for Mathematics Teaching and Learning

If mathematical proficiency is our desired outcome, and we believe that having a sense of number is explicitly linked to mathematical proficiency, then we need to clarify how we are going to structure learning experiences for mathematics teaching and learning. Number sense is our ultimate goal for our students, which allows them to make sense of the world through a numerate lens. (See Chapter 2 for an in-depth definition of number sense.) Figure 1.6 outlines a framework to use to plan for meaningful learning experiences with students.

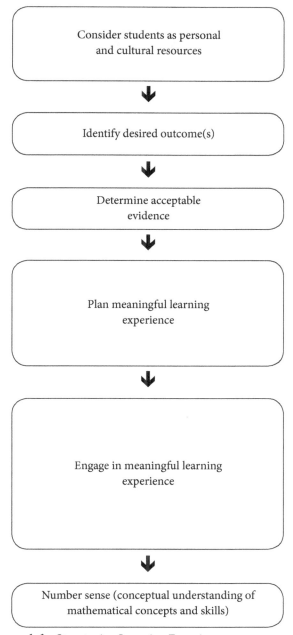

Figure 1.6: Framework for Structuring Learning Experiences

Essential Elements of Effective Practices

Many authors and researchers have identified the essential elements of effective practices to support the teaching and learning of mathematics (see Figure 1.7). These principles, dimensions, and practices, along with others, are frameworks for strengthening the teaching and learning of mathematics to enhance students' mathematical thinking. The individual components of the frameworks should not be taken in isolation; instead, together they constitute an approach to instruction and assessment that supports a vision for the teaching and learning of mathematics.

ESSENTIAL ELEMENTS TO SUPPORT TEACHING AND LEARNING MATHEMATICS			
Ten principles that underpin effective pedagogical practices to support student learning in mathematics (Anthony & Walshaw, 2009): 1. an ethic of care 2. arranging for learning 3. building on students' thinking 4. worthwhile mathematics tasks 5. making connections 6. assessment for learning 7. mathematical communication 8. mathematical language 9. tools and representations 10. teacher knowledge	*Ten interdisciplinary dimensions to strengthen and shift the teaching and learning of mathematics (McDougall, 2004):* 1. program scope and planning 2. meeting individual needs 3. learning environment 4. student tasks 5. constructing knowledge 6. communicating with parents 7. manipulatives and technology 8. students' mathematical communication 9. assessment 10. teacher knowledge and comfort with mathematics	*Eight practices to promote deep learning of mathematics (NCTM, 2014):* 1. Establish mathematical goals to focus learning. 2. Implement tasks that promote reasoning and problem solving. 3. Use and connect mathematical representations. 4. Facilitate meaningful mathematical discourse. 5. Pose purposeful questions. 6. Build procedural fluency from conceptual understanding. 7. Support productive struggle in learning mathematics. 8. Elicit and use evidence of student thinking.	*Four practices to help teachers design high-impact instruction to enhance student learning (Hattie et al., 2017):* 1. Make learning visible by balancing surface, deep, and transfer learning. 2. Make learning visible through teacher clarity (i.e., clarity of organizations, explanation, instruction, and assessment that is seen by students). 3. Make learning visible through appropriate mathematical tasks and mathematical talk. 4. Assess learning and provide feedback.

Figure 1.7

We have synthesized our understanding of these principles, dimensions, and practices and embedded them within the structure we developed to help you make connections to everyday teaching and learning (see Figure 1.8). Our goal is to explicitly connect these principles, dimensions, and practices to the actions that constitute meaningful learning for teaching and learning mathematics while focusing on what students need to exhibit or engage in. As we clarify our proposed structure, our focus will be on what teachers need to exhibit or engage in.

Consider students as personal and cultural resources	• Incorporate an ethic of care • Identify student strengths, interests, and learning preferences • Identify where students are along a mathematical progression • Incorporate knowledge of mathematics for teaching
⬇	
Identify desired outcome(s)	• Establish learning goals to focus learner • Consider program scope and planning
⬇	
Determine acceptable evidence	• Establish success criteria
⬇	
Plan meaningful learning experience	• Incorporate an ethic of care • Develop learning experiences that promote thinking and understanding • Arrange for learning • Build on student thinking • Consider surface, deep, and transfer learning
⬇	
Engage in meaningful learning experience	• Incorporate an ethic of care and teacher clarity • Promote mathematical talk and appropriate mathematical language • Incorporate the use of thinking tools • Support productive struggle • Elicit student thinking • Incorporate worthwhile learning experiences • Engage in assessment and provide feedback • Provide a learning environment • Encourage students to represent their thinking in a variety of ways
⬇	
Number sense (conceptual understanding of mathematical concepts and skills)	• Extend students' thinking • Communicate with parents

Figure 1.8: Framework for Structuring Learning Experiences and Actions that Create Meaningful Learning

Reflective Summary

A strong belief system about mathematics acts as a set of guiding principles for teachers as they approach teaching and learning in the classroom. Teaching and learning are so interwoven that it is difficult to separate one from the other. Simply stated, a student need is a teacher need. Teachers require many types of knowledge that will allow them to be responsive practitioners in a classroom: an understanding of what constitutes learning; an understanding of the process of how mathematics is learned over time; strong instructional pedagogy; and a deep understanding of each learner in the classroom. Students bring a breadth of knowledge, understanding, and experiences to the classroom. It is incumbent upon us, as teachers, to tap into these resources to leverage powerful learning opportunities in the classroom. Ultimately, we are educating students with the intent of creating productive, numerate citizens who can make sense of the world around them.

Teaching through Mathematical Thinking

Jonathan, a secondary school mathematics teacher, often reflects on his practice and how he might approach things differently to better support his students. In one particular class he uses a think-aloud strategy to model his thinking about developing an algebraic representation of a quadratic function given its graphical representation. At the end of the class, one of his students approaches him and says:

> "I think I get what you did to find the equation. It made sense that you started with the algebraic representation of $y = a\,(x - h)^2 + k$ because you had the vertex. And it wouldn't make sense to start with $y = a(x - r)(x - s)$ because the zeros weren't easy to get from the graph. So, I get that you would start there, now that you said it, and I think I can do that one too. But Sir, can you teach me how to think like you so I can do a think-aloud by myself first when the question is different? And Sir, when you ask us to 'think' about things, what is it exactly that you want us to do? Where do I even start so I can 'think'?"

Jonathan finds himself reflecting on the questions posed by the student, which leads him on a professional learning journey to help him make sense of the notion of thinking and what constitutes thinking—and more specifically, what constitutes mathematical thinking. The professional journey begins the following day. Jonathan asks his student if he can share his questions with the whole class so that, together, they can identify what constitutes thinking. They explore a number of questions as they collectively reflect on the think-aloud from the previous day. What is thinking? How do we know we are thinking? Where does the thinking begin when we are presented with a challenge? What mental actions support the thinking process? And how does thinking enhance our learning and understanding?

Opportunity for Reflection

How would you describe thinking? How would you describe mathematical thinking?

Thinking about Thinking

It is difficult to not get philosophical when we think about thinking. What is it that we are doing when we are thinking? More specifically, what does it mean for teachers and students? Thinking is an integral component of mathematics curricula and central to the teaching and learning of mathematics. It is also interesting to note that the word *think* ranks as the twelfth most-used word in the *Oxford English Dictionary*. But consider the following questions:

- When we ask our students to think as they engage with learning experiences, what is it that we are expecting them to do?
- When we are assessing students' thinking, what is it that we are looking for and listening for?

What Is Mathematical Thinking?

Simply stated, mathematical thinking includes mental actions and specific behaviors that students rely on as they engage in learning experiences designed to help them better understand mathematical concepts and skills and the role mathematics plays in the world around them. It is not thinking about the subject matter of mathematics, but rather a way of thinking about mathematical concepts and skills. Teaching through thinking supports learning with understanding, enabling students to solve the new kinds of problems they will inevitably face in the future. An emphasis on mathematical thinking influences the planning and execution of a learning experience. For example, using learning experiences that have multiple entry points and allow for the use of a variety of strategies, models, and/or questions that prompt further thinking supports teaching for mathematical thinking. Another example is organizing a lesson around one big idea of mathematics to elicit student thinking about various mathematical concepts.

Opportunity for Reflection

How else might the belief that mathematics is a way of thinking about things influence the planning or execution of a lesson?

Various researchers have developed frameworks to help support thinking classrooms. Figure 2.1 summarizes the different views of thinking and how they can be used to support the teaching and learning of mathematics.

THINKING FRAMEWORKS		
Pólya, 1945	Mason et al., 2010	Thomas, 2006
• Step 1: Understand the problem • Step 2: Make a plan • Step 3: Carry out the plan • Step 4: Look back at the solution.	• Phase 1: Entry (formulating the question precisely and deciding what to do) • Phase 2: Attack (resulting in the problem being solved) • Phase 3: Review (looking back at what has happened in order to improve and extend thinking)	• Talk about the problem with one another. • How can the problem be solved? • Identify a strategy for solving the problem. • Notice how your strategy helped you solve the problem. • Keep thinking about the problem.

Figure 2.1

Opportunity for Reflection

When we ask our students to think as they engage with learning experiences using the frameworks presented, what is that we are expecting them to do?

"No words are oftener on our lips than thinking and thought. So profuse and varied, indeed, is our use of these words that it is not easy to define just what we mean by them. . . . In its loosest sense, thinking signifies everything that, as we say, is in our heads or that goes through our minds." *Dewey, 1933, p. 5–6*

Although the frameworks outlined in Figure 2.1 present insights into thinking, we felt the need for further clarification. For example, what thinking actions support "understanding the problem"? What thinking actions are used when students are "attacking" or "reviewing" the problem? And what happens as students "keep thinking about the problem"?

This then begs the question, what goes through our minds as we engage in thinking? Fiore and Lebar (2017) describe what happens as we engage in thinking:

- inferring and interpreting
- analyzing
- evaluating
- making connections
- synthesizing
- reasoning and proving
- reflecting

They further propose *bigger ideas* to help teachers plan for meaningful learning experiences. These *bigger ideas* are mental actions or processes that help teachers and students make connections between the thinking skills to support mathematical thinking and the development of numerate learners (see Figure 2.2).

SUPPORTING MATHEMATICAL THINKING	
Thinking Skills	**Bigger Ideas**
Inferring and interpreting	• Making meaning and reaching an interpretation involves identifying stated and implied information and ideas. • Drawing meaning from explicit and implicit information requires use of prior knowledge and experiences. • Interpreting information and drawing a conclusion about it involves using reasoning to think about evidence, both stated and implied.
Making connections	• Understanding of texts, information, concepts, procedures, and skills is deepened through the use of prior knowledge, experiences, and opinions. • Gaining deeper meaning of concepts and skills occurs when relationships are identified and how they support understanding is explained. • Understanding is extended by comparing and contrasting information and ideas to one's own knowledge and experiences.
Analyzing	• Breaking down information involves identifying the parts of elements, and describing their purpose and function and how they contribute to meaning. • Determining how the parts or elements are connected to one another can be achieved by classifying, comparing, and contrasting information and ideas. • Inferring the relationship between the parts relies on using evidence to support generalizations, conclusions, and assumptions.
Evaluating	• Forming and defending opinions requires making judgments about information and ideas. • Justifying reasons for an informed decision involves using established criteria that help determine the validity and quality of information and ideas. • Assessing something's effectiveness involves using a set of criteria to draw conclusions about information, evidence, and ideas.
Synthesizing	• Combining and integrating ideas will lead to the creation of a new understanding. • Current understanding evolves and changes as more information and experiences are acquired. • Identifying when an understanding shifts and changes supports reasoning and proving.
Reasoning and proving	• Drawing conclusions for a justification involves inferring hypotheses and making conjectures. • Justifying one's thinking requires providing evidence that is reasonable and valid—that is, effective. • Being able to explain why conclusions and arguments are logical depends on evaluating the validity of proof.

Reflecting	• Thinking about one's own thought processes to acquire a deeper understanding of concepts allows monitoring of one's learning. • Analyzing and evaluating strategies used to improve learning enables assessment of one's understanding. • Thinking about how to expand knowledge or extend ability to make connections and gain understanding allows one to transfer learning to new contexts.

Figure 2.2

(Fiore & Lebar, 2017, p. 40–41)

"…mathematical thinking is not thinking about the subject matter of mathematics but a style of thinking that is a function of particular operation, processes, and dynamics recognizably mathematical." *Burton, 1984, p. 35*

When we tell someone we are thinking mathematically, what are we actually doing? There are varying but interconnected descriptions about what constitutes mathematical thinking (see Figure 2.3).

PERSPECTIVES ON MATHEMATICAL THINKING

Bryant, 1999	Mason et al., 2000	Burton, 1984
"Thinking mathematically changes ourselves. To think mathematically affects our being: that which is prior to our doing, and the ground of our choices and decisions." (p. 47)	"Mathematical thinking is driven by the exercise of mathematical powers such as: stressing and ignoring; specializing and generalizing; imagining and expressing; conjecturing and convincing; ordering and classifying; abstracting and instantiating." (p. 102)	The Processes of Mathematical Thinking: specializing, conjecturing, generalizing, and convincing

Figure 2.3

Opportunity for Reflection

You have had an opportunity to explore varying perspectives of mathematical thinking. How has your thinking shifted?

Identifying Mathematical Thinking

Now that we have further explored thinking and mathematical thinking, consider the following noticing and naming activity. As you reflect on the student solutions to the learning experience:
1. highlight evidence of students' mathematical thinking; and
2. describe how it represents mathematical thinking.

Learning Intentions: To engage in professional noticing to identify and interpret students' mathematical thinking.

Success Criteria:

You will:
- reflect on students' possible solutions
- describe mathematical thinking
- notice evidence of mathematical thinking
- interpret students' mathematical thinking

Learning Experience: Create a linear growing pattern. Describe how you know it is a linear growing pattern.

Student Solution #1:

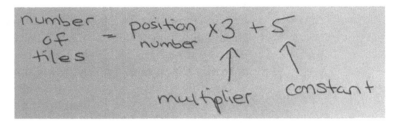

Student Solution #2:

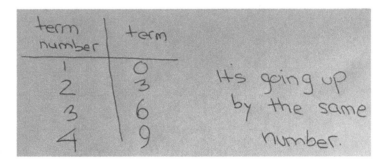

Student Solution #3:

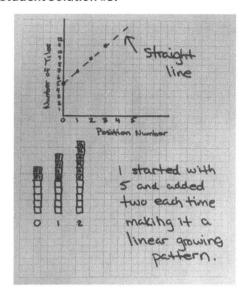

Figure 2.4 outlines the questions the teacher posed during the learning experience to further identify student thinking.

DOCUMENTATION OF STUDENT THINKING THROUGH MATH TALK	
Questions Posed by the Teacher	**Student Responses**
What mathematical ideas does this make you think of?	"I was asked to create a growing pattern, but it had to be linear, so I thought about making patterns."
What helped you select the strategy you used to represent your thinking?	"I remember learning about relationships, things like what is the relationship between the position number and the number of tiles."
How have you shown your mathematical thinking?	"I used two different color tiles, one to show the initial value of 5 that stayed the same, and the other to show how much my pattern grew by each time."
Could you show your thinking in another way?	"I could use a graph."

What was the most challenging part of the task? Why?	"The only part that confused me was the position number of 0 … that kind of didn't make sense to me … but it kind of did because it was where I started and the next one was 7."
How do you know your answer is correct?	"I know my thinking makes sense because both things are saying the same thing but in a different way … and you can see that both are growing by 2 and both form straight lines … so I know it is a linear growing pattern."
Is there anything you are curious about?	"I am wondering if I could think of a real-life example I could use that would make sense."

Figure 2.4

Consolidating the Learning Experience: Reflect on the learning intentions by considering the following questions:
- How are the student solutions similar? Different?
- What helped you make interpretations after you highlighted the mathematical thinking?
- Which solutions showed more evidence of mathematical thinking? What makes you say that?
- What are you still curious about?

A Synthesis of Our Understanding about Mathematical Thinking

As addressed in the overview of thinking skills and bigger ideas in Figure 2.2, the thinking skill of synthesizing involves combining and integrating new ideas to develop a new understanding. As a result, we felt it would make sense for us to synthesize our understanding of mathematical thinking (see Figure 2.5). We recognize that there is an overlap in the descriptors, but note that the intentions are slightly different. For example, as students engage in reflection as they work with a learning experience (action), they are thinking about previous learning experiences and about their own thought processes to monitor their own learning. In contrast, as students engage in reflection after they have worked with the learning experience (outcome), they are thinking about how to expand their newfound knowledge and understanding and transfer it to new contexts (Fiore & Lebar, 2017).

OUR UNDERSTANDING OF MATHEMATICAL THINKING	
Mathematical Thinking as an Action	**Mathematical Thinking as an Outcome**
• Inferring and interpreting • Analyzing • Evaluating • Reflecting • Looking for patterns • Making connections • Making conjectures • Recognizing relationships • Identifying and incorporating appropriate mathematical knowledge and skills needed to solve a problem • Representing • Reasoning	• Making generalizations • Seeing mathematics as a connected whole as opposed to isolated concepts and skills • Justifying with evidence • Drawing conclusions • Applying knowledge and understanding of mathematical concepts and skills • Being a reflective learner • Synthesizing • Having a sense of mathematical concepts and skills

Figure 2.5

Making Sense of Number through Mathematical Thinking

"Above all, number sense is characterized by a desire to make sense of numerical situations, including relating numbers to context and analyzing the effect of manipulations on numbers. It is a way of thinking that should permeate all aspects of mathematics teaching and learning." *Reys, 1994, p. 114*

When students have made sense of mathematics concepts and skills by engaging in mathematical thinking, it can be said that students have made sense of number or have *number sense*. In a nutshell, number sense is an intuitive way of thinking about mathematical concepts and their various uses in meaningful and flexible ways (Markovits & Sowder, 1994).

Number sense is a perspective from which to view the teaching and learning of mathematics. When students share the perspective of learning mathematics for number sense, they rely on mathematical thinking to build understanding. When teachers share the perspective of teaching mathematics for number sense, they embrace meaningful learning environments that provide students with opportunities to deepen their conceptual understanding of mathematics concepts and skills.

Teachers and students view themselves as co-learners and active participants when teaching and learning for number sense (see Figure 2.6).

TEACHING AND LEARNING FOR NUMBER SENSE ROLES

Teacher's Role	Students' Role
• Considers students as personal and cultural resources. • Makes links to the curriculum. • Aligns assessment to instruction that is differentiated. • Incorporates opportunities for accountable talk. • Promotes inquiry-based learning. • Provides engaging learning experiences that promote mathematical thinking. • Allows for the use of multiple thinking tools and representations. • Uses effective questions to elicit student thinking and prompt further learning. • Promotes learning for understanding. • Considers students' learning needs to guide their personal professional learning. • Believes in their ability to enhance student thinking and learning.	• Rely on *mathematical thinking* to make sense of mathematical concepts and skills. • Believe in their ability as mathematical thinkers and learners. • Engage in accountable talk. • Pose questions to further their thinking. • Use thinking tools to develop their understanding and represent their thinking. • Apply their mathematical knowledge and understanding to new contexts. • Value learning as a process and not an outcome. • Rely on their intuitive feeling for numbers.

Figure 2.6

(Reys, 1994)

Intuition and Mathematical Thinking

"By establishing a classroom atmosphere that encourages exploration, thinking, and discussion, and by selecting appropriate problems and activities, the teacher can cultivate number sense during all mathematical experiences." *Reys, 1994, p. 120*

Students who exhibit number sense have an intuitive feeling for numbers (McIntosh et al., 1992). The *Oxford English Dictionary* describes *intuition* as the ability to understand something instinctively, without the need for conscious reasoning. Piaget used the term *intuitive thought* to describe the knowledge young children realize they have but are unaware of how they know it. For example, a child demonstrates intuitive thinking when they identify the pail on the left holds more sand.

Number sense builds on students' natural intuition and convinces them that mathematics is about understanding and not just using a collection of rules. The outcome of number sense includes:

- using numbers flexibly when mentally computing, estimating, and making mathematical judgments (e.g., judging the reasonableness of an answer);
- moving between various representations;
- relating numbers and operations; and
- understanding mathematical properties (e.g., commutative property, associative property, distributive property).

(Adapted from Reys, 1994; Markovits & Sowder, 1994)

"Number sense can be described as good intuition about numbers and their relationships. It develops gradually as a result of exploring numbers, visualizing them in a variety of contexts, and relating them in ways that are not limited by traditional algorithms." *Howden, 1989, p. 11*

Opportunity for Reflection

How does the following narrative demonstrate an intuition about number? *Stella is sitting with a group of teachers exploring algebraic reasoning. She is sitting with her mentor, Wendy, a thoughtful and caring teacher who demonstrates a voracious appetite for learning. The session is engaging, with lots of time for teachers to talk about and reflect on math. Stella has been exploring addition and subtraction for much of the morning when the facilitator presents the following task:*

What is the sum of these numbers?

1	2	3	4
5	6	7	8
9	10	11	12
13	14	15	16
17	18	19	20

Stella notices her mentor, Wendy, is exceptionally quick to approach the task. She quietly observes Wendy's strategy for finding the sum. Stella sees that Wendy quickly and methodically starts at 1 and adds 2, then adds 3 to that sum, then 4, and so on, until she has added 20 to her running total. Wendy's addition is flawless and she finds the sum of 210 a few minutes later. Stella knows that Wendy's instinct in most avenues of her professional life is to carefully consider the situation, make connections to her own practice, and then offer a reasoned opinion. However, Wendy's instinct when approaching a math task is to compute the numbers in the order they are presented. Making a mental note to think more about this later, Stella works through the task herself. She creates sets of 21 by adding 1 and 20, 19 and 2, 18 and 3, and so on, until she has 10 sets of 21. She quickly finds the product of 21 and 10 as 210. This situation becomes a milestone moment in Stella's career. Wendy's strategy was successful; however, her instinct or intuition was to jump straight to computing. Stella wonders how she can get her students to change their instincts to carefully consider the task at hand and to look for efficiencies and patterns before computing.

Number Sense and Critical Thinking

As discussed in Chapter 1, the teaching of mathematics requires that we have different types of knowledge: knowledge of students, knowledge of pedagogy, and knowledge of mathematics for teaching. It also requires us to plan for meaningful learning experiences that provide students with opportunities to develop number sense and mathematical ways of thinking about things as a basis for solving problems they may encounter in the real world. The learning intentions of mathematics education include teaching for mathematical thinking and critical thinking to enhance student understanding of mathematical concepts and skills (Jacobs et al., 2010; Jaworkski, 2015). We have already explored thinking and mathematical thinking; next, we will touch upon critical thinking.

Critical thinking is often framed as a set of generic thinking and reasoning skills where the outcome is described as a basis for decision making and problem solving. As addressed in Chapter 1, the National Research Council (2001) defines the learning of mathematics as five interrelated strands: conceptual understanding, procedural fluency, strategic competence, adaptive reasoning, and productive disposition—critical thinking and mathematical thinking are embedded within each of the strands. Critical mathematical thinking is considered a by-product of meaningful learning experiences and mathematical thinking. The Ontario Ministry of Education (2012) describes thinking as the ability to "access, manage, create, and evaluate information in order to think imaginatively and critically to solve problems and make decisions, including those related to issues of fairness, equity, and social justice" (p. 12). The latter part of this definition addresses the element of critical mathematical thinking.

As with mathematical thinking, there are varying perspectives on what constitutes critical thinking (see Figure 2.7).

PERSPECTIVES ON CRITICAL THINKING		
Brookhart, 2010	Chance, 1986	Jablonka, 2014
Critical thinking is reasoning so that we can make informed decisions about what to believe and what to do.	Critical thinking is the ability to analyze facts, generate and organize ideas, defend opinions, make comparisons, draw inferences, evaluate arguments, and solve problems.	Critical thinking is a reflective thought process that we rely on to make judgments and informed decisions.

Figure 2.7

In mathematics education literature, there is a large overlap between mathematical reasoning, problem solving, and critical thinking. However, there is common agreement that critical thinking does not automatically emerge as a by-product of any mathematics curriculum. Instead, it is the outcome of learning experiences that draw on students' contributions and afford processes of reasoning and questions when students collaboratively engage in rich tasks. In other words, critical thinking is about learning how to think, not what to think.

The Foundation for Critical Thinking has adopted Scriven and Paul's (1987) description of critical thinking:

"Critical thinking is the intellectually disciplined process of actively and skillfully conceptualizing, applying, analyzing, synthesizing, and/or evaluating information gathered from, or generated by, observation, experience, reflection, reasoning, or communication, as a guide to belief and action. In its exemplary form, it is based universal intellectual values that transcend subject matter division: clarity, accuracy, precision, consistency, relevance, sound evidence, good reasons, breadth, and fairness."

Critical Thinking and the Numerate Learner

Efforts to enhance students' critical thinking skills in mathematics continue to elicit conversations among educators and researchers. The development of critical thinking skills encourages students to think independently and make informed decisions in the context of everyday life, and it can improve student achievement in mathematics (Silver & Kenney, 1995; Jacob, 2012). As students engage in mathematical problem solving, critical thinking is analytical thinking and reflection that involves questioning, connecting, and evaluating all aspects of the problem (Krulick & Rudnick, 1995). In the context for our vision for teaching and learning mathematics, engaging in critical mathematical thinking supports the development of the numerate learner. Numerate learners apply their sense of number to better understand the world around them so they can participate as reflective and competent citizens in a rapidly changing world (Fiore & Lebar, 2017).

As shown in Figure 2.8, to become numerate, students must learn to *make sense* of mathematical concepts and skills, *use* mathematical skills effectively, *communicate* mathematical thinking clearly, and *critically interpret* texts, using mathematical knowledge and skills. When students become numerate, they apply their sense of number and see mathematics as a way of thinking about cross-curricular ideas and not as a series of isolated topics or skills. For teachers, the Four Roles of the Numerate Learner framework supports an integrated approach for effective mathematics assessment and instruction that fosters mathematical thinking and promotes numeracy development (Fiore & Lebar, 2016).

It is important to note that we are not using *numeracy* and *mathematics* interchangeably. Mathematics, like language, is the basis for thinking, understanding, and communicating. Numeracy, on the other hand, refers to using number sense and recognizing how our knowledge and understanding of mathematics concepts and skills help us to better understand the world. The Four Roles of the Numerate Learner provides an avenue for educators to view the mathematics curriculum through a different lens as they plan for meaningful learning experiences that foster mathematical thinking.

Sense Maker	**Skill User**
Makes sense of mathematical patterns, operations, computations, procedures, relationships, and language. A *sense maker* applies knowledge and understanding of mathematical concepts to a variety of contexts. Both procedural fluency and conceptual understanding are being developed and consolidated.	Recognizes and knows when and how to apply number operations, computational strategies, and procedures. A *skill user* uses mathematical conventions and vocabulary to express and organize ideas and mathematical thinking. Procedural fluency is being developed.

Sense Maker

Makes sense of mathematical patterns, operations, computations, procedures, relationships, and language. A *sense maker* applies knowledge and understanding of mathematical concepts to a variety of contexts. Both procedural fluency and conceptual understanding are being developed and consolidated.

- Does this answer make sense to you?
- What is this question asking you to do? What words or phrases make you think that?
- Where have you seen this before?
- How would you represent the data? (Examples: numerically, geometrically, algebraically, pictorially, graphically)
- How can you represent this in a different way?
- How do these representations compare? How are they different?
- What are the similarities and differences between these two numbers?
- What is the pattern? How do you know?
- If you continue the pattern, what will be the next term?
- Can you identify a rule for the pattern? Explain your thinking.

Skill User

Recognizes and knows when and how to apply number operations, computational strategies, and procedures. A *skill user* uses mathematical conventions and vocabulary to express and organize ideas and mathematical thinking. Procedural fluency is being developed.

- What does that word mean? (Examples: *sum*, *product*, *ratio*, *mean*, *median*, *mode*)
- What patterns do you see?
- Which number is biggest?
- What mathematical operations are you going to use?
- Determine the value of the variable.
- Simplify the expression.
- Organize data into categories (e.g., based on qualities such as color or favorite food).
- How do you represent parallel lines?
- How can you represent equal line segments?

The Numerate Learner

Thought Communicator

Communicates mathematical thinking through problem solving, reasoning and proving, reflecting, using thinking tools, connecting, and representing to gain a deeper understanding of mathematical concepts.

- Explain how you would find the 10th term of the pattern and justify your answer.
- Explain and share the results of the survey you designed.
- Select and justify the unit that you think should be used to measure the perimeter.
- Here is the answer. What could the question be? Justify your response.
- Given these two different solutions, determine which solution is correct and explain your thinking.
- Provide a counter-example to represent your thinking.
- How does your solution compare to and contrast with your partner's?
- Create a poem, song, or dance to demonstrate your understanding.

Critical Interpreter

Adopts a critical numeracy lens to apply mathematical knowledge and skills to challenge the power in the usage of numbers, patterns, measurements, graphs, shapes, figures, pictures, and/or statistics (e.g., using a critical numeracy lens in real-life situations to examine the role mathematics plays in the world and the bias and perspective of those using the numeracy).

- Who might benefit from using these numbers in this context?
- Can you use data to support your argument or illustrate your ideas?
- Can you use data to support your critical stance?
- Can you use mathematical knowledge to question data? (Example: biased statistics on child poverty)
- Is the mathematical thinking represented fairly? Are there other perspectives that need to be considered?
- Identify the bias in this representation of data.

Figure 2.8: The Four Roles of the Numerate Learner

(Fiore & Lebar, 2017, p. 29)

Promoting Number Sense

Now that we have set the context, we will explore key number concepts in an effort to promote number sense. The suggested learning experiences presented in Chapters 3–6 reflect a set of principles that underpin effective practices to support the teaching and learning of mathematics by:

- invoking an ethic of care;
- arranging for learning so students can make sense of ideas independently and collaboratively;
- building on students' thinking;
- incorporating meaningful mathematics texts;
- providing students with opportunities to make connections;
- incorporating assessment practices that support student learning;
- providing opportunities for mathematical communication;
- fostering students' use and understanding of mathematical language;
- drawing on a range of representations and tools to support students' mathematical development; and

- providing teachers with sound knowledge as a basis for initiating learning and responding to the mathematical needs of all their students.

(Anthony & Walshaw, 2009)

These learning experiences allow students to make sense of mathematical concepts and skills across the various strands, with clearly outlined learning intentions and success criteria linked to the *important stuff*. They make clear what we want students to learn for that learning experience and include what it is we know about our learners and what we want our learners to know. The success criteria help us to identify successful attainment of the learning intentions and allow students to engage confidently in the learning. Authentic student solutions are incorporated and triangulated evidence of thinking and successful learning are highlighted. Specific teacher thinking about students' thinking is also included to inform next steps.

The intent of Chapters 3–6 is for you to further deepen your understanding of key number concepts so you can plan for learning experiences that enable students to make sense of mathematical concepts and skills (see Figure 2.9). By examining the curriculum through the development of the key number concepts, you will foster meaningful learning environments that promote mathematical thinking across the strands.

OVERVIEW OF KEY NUMBER CONCEPTS TO PROMOTE NUMBER SENSE

Number Concept	The Important Stuff
Quantity	<ul><li>Numbers tell how much or how many.</li><li>The ability to subitize (i.e., to instantly recognize an amount without counting) is an efficient way of determining how much or how many.</li><li>The number of objects remains the same even when rearranged.</li><li>Estimation is useful to get a sense of the size of a number.</li><li>The same number can represent different values in different contexts.</li><li>Quantities are represented using numbers, while the place of a digit in a number determines its value.</li><li>Some mathematical models relate number to space and help make sense of how big a number is.</li><li>You can use more than one number to describe the same situation.</li><li>You can operate on quantities to make new quantities.</li><li>You can describe the relative size of a number with fractions, decimals, and/or percents.</li></ul>

Counting	<ul><li>The counting principles help us to count with meaning.</li><li>Counting strategies are useful when performing operations with numbers.</li><li>Counting tells us how many are in a set.</li></ul> *Counting principles:* <ul><li>There is one and only one number said for each object (One-to-One Principle).</li><li>There is a consistent set of counting words that never changes (Stable Order Principle).</li><li>The last number spoken tells how many (Cardinal Principle).</li><li>It does not matter what you count; the process for counting remains the same (Abstraction Principle).</li><li>It does not matter in which order you count; the number in the set does not change (Order Relevance Principle).</li></ul>
Relating	<ul><li>Classifying numbers provides information about the characteristics of numbers.</li><li>Benchmark numbers are useful for relating and estimating number.</li><li>Addition and subtraction are intrinsically related.</li><li>Multiplication and division are intrinsically related.</li><li>The relationship between two numbers can be described additively or multiplicatively.</li><li>Understanding the relationship between quantities helps to make generalizations and can be expressed as algebraic expressions and equations.</li><li>There are many ways to describe the relationship between numbers.</li></ul>
Representing	<ul><li>Representations help to make abstract thinking visible.</li><li>Reasoning with representations helps to generalize.</li><li>Representing is a way of communicating thinking and understanding.</li><li>Multiple representations provide opportunities to make connections between the different ways of thinking about things.</li><li>Different representations tell us different things about mathematical thoughts.</li><li>There are different ways to represent mathematical thoughts.</li><li>Different representations can be useful for different purposes</li></ul>

Figure 2.9

Quantity

Amanda values community in the classroom and often provides a morning challenge or game for her students to play upon entry. Students have been investigating whole numbers and she wants them thinking about quantity. In today's card game, students are trying to make the smallest possible three-digit number using three cards. Each student receives a playing board with three rectangular boxes in a row and a pile of playing cards with the 10s, jacks, queens, and kings removed. Playing in pairs or trios, students take turns drawing one playing card from the deck and placing it face-up on their playing board. Once a card is placed on the board, it cannot be moved. Amanda notices that Kavish has created the number 149 and investigates his thinking.

Amanda: "Kavish, will you tell me about your strategy for placing your cards?"

Kavish: "Sure, I tried to put bigger digits on this side (pointing to the right side of his game board) and put smaller digits on this side (pointing to the left side of his game board)."

Amanda: "Why does your strategy make sense?"

Kavish: "I want the smaller digits to be first so that the number is smaller. See, I have a 1 here, it makes 100, I have a 4 here and it makes 40, and I have a 9 here and it makes 9. Together they make 149."

Amanda: "I think you are saying that this 1 has a value of 100, this 4 has a value of 40, and this 9 has a value of 9. Is that what you are saying?"

Kavish: "Yes."

Amanda: "How is it possible that a 1 can have a value more than a 9?

Kavish: "The 1 is in the hundreds place and the 9 is in the ones place."

Amanda: "In what situations does a 1 have more value than a 9?"

Kavish: (Pausing to think) "If a 1 is to the left of a 9 in a number then the 1 has more value than a 9."

Amanda: (Turning to both Kavish and his partner) "Can either of you think of a situation where this is not true?"

Amanda has clear learning goals for her students who are playing this game. She has created a situation where her students can make sense of quantity and formalize place value ideas by pushing them toward the important generalization that the place of a digit in a number determines its value.

THE IMPORTANT STUFF

- Numbers tell how much or how many.
- The ability to subitize (i.e., to instantly recognize an amount without counting) is an efficient way of determining how much or how many.
- The number of objects remains the same even when rearranged.
- Estimation is useful to get a sense of the size of a number.
- The same number can represent different values in different contexts.
- Quantities are represented using numbers, while the place of a digit in a number determines its value.
- Some mathematical models relate number to space and help make sense of how big a number is.
- You can use more than one number to describe the same situation.
- You can operate on quantities to make new quantities.
- You can describe the relative size of a number with fractions, decimals, and/or percent.

Making Sense of Quantity

Simply stated, quantity tells how many. Children begin to recognize and make sense of quantity at a very young age by recognizing very small whole numbers. They develop a more sophisticated understanding over time. Ultimately, we strive to ensure that students gain an understanding of very large numbers into the hundreds of thousands and millions in context, while also having a strong sense of very small numbers including negative integers, fractions, decimals, and percent. Students generally develop a sense of quantity over time as follows:
- Recognizes and makes very small quantities.
- Perceptually subitizes common number patterns (e.g., instantly recognizes "3" on the face of a number cube).
- Conceptually subitizes common number patterns (e.g., "5" on a number cube is two groups of two and one in the middle) and understand that there are numbers inside of numbers (e.g., there is a 5 and 2 inside of 7).
- Derives quantities by using other known quantities (e.g., 5 + 5= 10 so 5 + 6 = 11 because 5 + 5 is the same as 5 + 5 + 1).
- Develops flexible strategies to operate on smaller then bigger numbers.
- Develops a sense of increasingly greater whole numbers over time.
- Identifies and interprets increasingly sophisticated fractions (e.g., proper, improper, mixed numbers).
- Uses fractions, decimals, and percent interchangeably.

(Clements & Samara, 2014; Small, 2005)

Many children come to school with an inherent understanding of small numbers and can quickly recognize small collections. In their book, *Elementary and Middle School Mathematics*, Van de Walle and colleagues outline four important number relationships that primary school teachers should emphasize to create strong mathematical foundations:

1. spatial relationships (recognizing common number patterns quickly without having to count);
2. 1 or 2 more or less;
3. relating numbers to anchors of 5 and 10; and
4. parts/whole relationships.

Each of the first three number relationships helps to support student understanding of the fourth number relationship—parts/whole relationships. Early instruction with a combined focus on developing these number relationships and helping students to make connections among them will empower students to develop number sense over time.

Using Models to Support Understanding of Quantity

Models are a powerful way to explore numbers and help students make connections between representations. (We will explore different ways to represent numbers and mathematical thoughts in Chapter 6.) It is worth noting here that some models and representations of numbers are especially helpful to develop early number sense. Research has demonstrated that an increasing reliance on linear representations of numbers plays an important role in the development of numerical knowledge (Ramani & Siegler, 2008) (see Figure 3.1). The ability to equate number to space plays a powerful function in helping students develop a sense of number. As such, an emphasis on developing students' understanding of a number line will support linear representations and should be prioritized over less effective models. Other research demonstrates the importance of developing number lines over time, but also has found that number paths are usually more developmentally appropriate for students until around Grade 2 (Fuson et al., 2007).

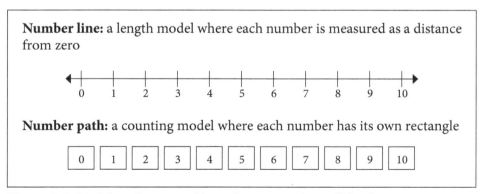

Figure 3.1: Models to Represent Linear Representations of Numbers

As students develop strategies and big ideas over time, it is important to introduce models that will help students extend and consolidate their understanding. Exploring numbers in many contexts plays a central role in the teaching and learning of number sense. How students are introduced to numbers helps them to clarify their understanding, make connections, and gain flexibility with numbers. For example, the models in Figure 3.2 can be used to help support students' understanding of early number relationships.

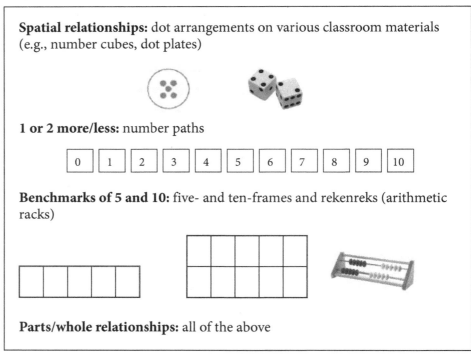

Spatial relationships: dot arrangements on various classroom materials (e.g., number cubes, dot plates)

1 or 2 more/less: number paths

Benchmarks of 5 and 10: five- and ten-frames and rekenreks (arithmetic racks)

Parts/whole relationships: all of the above

Figure 3.2: Models to Support Understanding of Number Relationships

"For a model to be powerful, it needs to have the potential to become, over time, a powerful tool for thinking." *Fosnot, 2014*

Introducing models in context is a powerful strategy to help students make sense of the model. The eventual goal is to develop models in such a way that students use them as powerful tools for thinking. Different models can be used to reveal different things about a number. Consider the three models for a quantity of 7 shown in Figure 3.3.

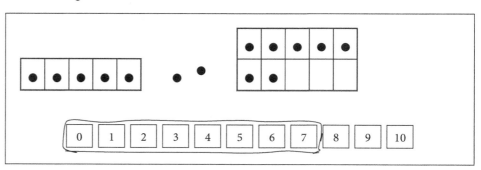

Figure 3.3: Models Showing a Quantity of 7

Under the teacher's careful guidance, students use models to explore number. Each of the three models in Figure 3.3 helps students to explore 7 and helps to highlight different things. The five-frame supports the idea that 7 is 2 more than 5, while the ten-frame shows that you need 3 more to get to 10. In both of these situations, students are developing a sense of anchors of 5 and 10. When students use a number path to consider 7, with prompting, they will see that 7 is 1 more than 6 and 1 less than 8, leading them to develop understanding of the relationship of 1 or 2 more or less. With a growing familiarity with models, students will begin to use them to demonstrate their own thinking, eventually leading to students creating a mental version of the model that can be accessed as a tool for thinking as needed (see Figure 3.4).

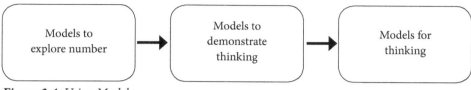

Figure 3.4: Using Models

Opportunity for Reflection

What models are you introducing to your students to help them make sense of quantity? When is the "right" time to introduce each model?

Using Prompting to Think About Quantity

The purpose of interactions between teachers and students is "... more about the development of the young mathematician than it is about the arrival at an answer to the problem, or correcting the mathematics on the page" (Imm et al., 2012, p. 28). In other words, the purpose of interactions with students is to notice, interpret, confirm, and respond to the learner. It is important that we use precious time with our students to help clarify their understanding of quantity and then nudge them further down a progression for learning. We want students to notice interesting things about numbers, make conjectures, test to see if there are other situations where this is true, and make generalizations about things they have noticed. Consider how the thinking stems and prompting questions identified below can be applied to a wide range of opportunities across different math strands.

Thinking stems:

I can show this number by . . .
When I make a number this way, it shows me . . . about this number.
If . . . happens, then . . . will also happen.
This model shows . . . about the number . . . .
My estimate is . . .; it makes sense because . . . .

Prompting questions:

What is the biggest number you know?
When is . . . a big number? When is . . . a small number?
How can a number that starts with a 9 be smaller than a number that starts with 1?
What model helps you to show what . . . means?
What number is too big? Too small? Your best guess? Why? (estimation)
What strategy did you use to estimate?
What do you know about that number?

How Will We Know Our Students Understand Quantity?

We will know that our students are determining and understanding quantity when we hear or see them doing the following:

- ☐ Estimating the magnitude of a number using a variety of strategies, including visualizing and using their own schema.
- ☐ Using a variety of strategies to determine quantity (e.g., counting, one-to-one correspondence).
- ☐ Recognizing common number arrangements quickly.
- ☐ Understanding that there are smaller numbers hidden inside of bigger numbers.
- ☐ Using really big quantities and really small quantities (e.g., fractions and decimals) in real contexts and then abstractly.
- ☐ Using an open number line to show any number.
- ☐ Determining that numbers go on forever and why they go on forever.
- ☐ Explaining and using negative numbers.
- ☐ Using place value to talk about the value of each digit in a number.
- ☐ Performing operations on quantities to make new quantities.

The progression shown in Figure 3.5 demonstrates a simplified version of how children develop a sense of quantity over time as they move from foundational understandings to more sophisticated understandings. It is possible and likely that students will be working in more than one phase at a time. Although synthesized from research, this progression is an approximation of how students might develop over time and is not intended to be a fulsome picture.

- Uses ordinal and cardinal numbers with smaller whole numbers.
- Conserves number.
- Understands $\frac{1}{2}$ in different contexts.

- Uses ordinal and cardinal numbers with whole numbers.
- Groups quantities to skip count to tell how many.
- Understands fractions of a region for common fractions.
- Uses base 10 models for two-digit numbers.

- Uses numbers up to 1,000 in context.
- Identifies and creates fractions of a region or of a set for simple fractions.
- Uses decimals with tenths and hundredths.
- Applies base 10 models into thousands and hundredths.

- Relates numbers proportionally.
- Uses numbers into the millions in context and negative numbers.
- Identifies and creates fractions of a region or set for proper then improper fractions.
- Equates numbers between 0 and 1 as a fraction, decimal, or percent.
- Identifies patterns in the number system involving large whole numbers and decimals to the thousandths.

Figure 3.5: *Sample Progression for Quantity*

(Adapted from Small, 2005; Clements & Sarama, 2014)

Learning Experiences

The following learning experiences are organized into grade bands: Kindergarten–Grade 2, Grade 3–5, and Grade 6–10. They are designed to demonstrate how you can use your students as resources to plan for and deliver responsive tasks based on a sample progression of learning. We have used learning experiences from across the strands of mathematics to help key number ideas emerge.

Kindergarten–Grade 2 Learning Experience #1

Learning Intentions: To get a sense of the size of numbers in many different situations.

Success Criteria:

Students will

- establish the quantity of a collection using a strategy that makes sense for the situation
- explain and defend the strategy they used to find a quantity
- make connections between quantities

What I know about my learner	What I want my learner to know
<ul><li>Counts the objects in a small collection by ones and understands that the last number said is the number in the collection.</li><li>Describes where the second and third object (and others) are in a line and how the ordinal number changes if you start from a different place.</li><li>Quickly identifies that the number in a collection remains the same if the objects are rearranged or spread out without recounting.</li><li>Identifies and shows half in different situations.</li><li>Solves addition and subtraction problems by counting three times.</li></ul>	<ul><li>Group objects in a collection to count more efficiently while maintaining accuracy.</li><li>Use a known quantity to find an unknown quantity.</li><li>Generalize the use of both ordinal and cardinal numbers to larger whole numbers.</li><li>Divide wholes into parts and use a unit fraction to describe each regional part.</li><li>Understand that the digit 2 in the number 23 has a value of 2 tens or 20, and the 3 has a value of 3 ones or 3.</li><li>Develop a wider bank of addition and subtraction strategies and choose one that works for the situation.</li></ul>

Learning Experience
Choose a number of pictures you might see on a pictograph. Show what the graph might look like. Use numbers and other words to tell lots of things about your graph.

Student thinking:	Teacher thinking:
Saying: • *I think we should draw 20 pictures on the pictograph, one for each student in the class.* • (Whispers the number of pictures while counting using the sequence.) *1, 2, 3, 4, . . .* • *Soccer is the most, baseball is the smallest.* *Doing:* • Draws a few pictures onto the graph; stops after drawing five and counts the number drawn. • Adds three more pictures onto the graph; stops and counts the total number starting from one. • Repeats by adding a few pictures at a time and recounting until 20 pictures have been drawn. *Representing:* 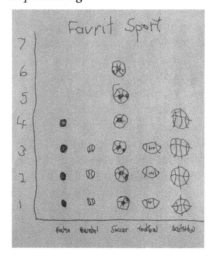	*Noticing:* • Counts using conventional sequence. • Identifies the quantity of the collection as the last number said in the sequence. • Orders numbers from smallest to greatest and vice versa. • Uses "ball" pictures to represent a sport. • Uses an appropriate title, label, and spacing of the symbols. *Interpreting:* • Uses one-to-one tagging when counting with accuracy. • Understands magnitude by identifying the total as the last number said in the counting sequence. • Understands relative quantity using "most" and "smallest." *Confirming:* • *What did you do?* • *How did you know when you got to 20 pictures?* • *What steps did you use?* *Responding:* • *What would happen if I moved these three to this column? What would be the total number of pictures?* • *How else could you count the objects?* • *How could you use one of the columns to help you decide how many are in a different column?*

Kindergarten–Grade 2 Learning Experience #2

Learning Intentions: To show how a number changes when you add to or subtract from it.

Success Criteria:

Students will

- establish a quantity as a result of joining or separating numbers
- estimate the result using reasoning
- notice patterns in the number system

What I know about my learner	What I want my learner to know
• Places objects into groups in order to skip count by 2s, 5s, and 10s to determine the quantity. • Uses ordinal and cardinal numbers to describe real-life contexts of two-digit numbers. • Divides shapes into common fractions, including quarters, and identifies halves and doubles of numbers. • Has developed a bank of strategies to add and subtract numbers under 100, including counting on. • Understands that 4 + 2 has the same sum as 2 + 4.	• Arrange objects into arrays. • Use knowledge of quantity to estimate with reasoning when operating on numbers. • Relate decimals to common fractions. • Understand that the digit 2 in the number 23 has a value of 2 tens or 20 and the 3 has a value of 3 ones or 3. • Identify patterns in the number system that will help them operate on quantities.

Learning Experience	
You overhear someone say, "This one is 10 paperclips longer than that one." What might they have been measuring? How long is each?	

Student thinking:	Teacher thinking:
Saying: • *This pencil is 3 paperclips long, so I need to find something that is 4, 5, 6, 7, 8, 9, 10, 11, 12, 13 paper clips long.* (counting on fingers) • *The carpet is way too long and a book is too short. Maybe a desk will work.* • *2, 4, 6, 8, 10, 12, 13 . . . the desk is 13 paperclips.*	*Noticing:* • Naturally uses skip counting to determine the quantity in a group. • Understands that you should use a common unit when measuring. • Uses schema and visualizes to help make estimates.

Doing:
- Collects several items from around the classroom and a box of paperclips.
- Sorts the paperclips by size.
- Lays out 10 paperclips end-to-end.
- Touches each paperclip while counting.

Representing:

Interpreting:
- Chooses to skip count because it is more efficient than counting by ones and grouping by another number does not fit the context.
- Understands several of the principles of measurement.
- Lines up 10 paperclips to get a sense of how much longer one object has to be than the other.

Confirming:
- *What did you do?*
- *What advice would you give someone who wants to compare the measurements of two objects?*
- *How did you decide which objects might work?*

Responding:
- *How are the numbers 3 and 13 the same? How are they different?*
- *In what other situations do you think that might be true?*
- *If an object is 15 paperclips long, how long do you think an object would be that is 10 paperclips longer?*

Additional Learning Experiences to Support Learning Quantity

- You are measuring two shapes. One shape is bigger in one way and smaller in a different way than the other shape. What might the shapes look like? Tell how you know you are right.
- What is a pretty big number that you know? How could you show that it is pretty big?
- (Provide colored tiles for students.) Show a shape with a big perimeter. Tell the perimeter.
- You can hold a lot of something in your hand. What could it be? How many do you think you can hold? Tell why you are right.

Grade 3–5 Learning Experience # 1

Learning Intentions: To show that the same quantity can take many different forms.

Success Criteria:

Students will

- establish the quantity of a regional part using a strategy that makes sense for the situation
- demonstrate that the area of a regional part remains the same when the whole and the unit fraction are the same
- count fractions

What I know about my learner	What I want my learner to know
• Skip counts forwards and backwards by different numbers to establish a quantity. • Relates numbers into the hundreds to real-life contexts. • Equates decimals in common real-life contexts. • Identifies common unit fractions. • Can name the value of each digit in a two- and three-digit number.	• Count forwards and backwards by decimals and fractions to determine quantities. • Relate numbers into the thousands to real life contexts. • Equate decimal tenths to an area of $\frac{1}{10}$ the size of the whole or a distance of $\frac{1}{10}$ of the total distance. • Identify fractions as a number of unit fractions (e.g., $\frac{3}{4}$ is three one-fourths). • Rename whole numbers to 1,000 (e.g., 1,000 is 10 hundreds or 100 tens).

Learning Experience Draw three or more identical regular polygons. Divide each polygon into $\frac{1}{4}$s in different ways. Convince a friend you are right.	
Student thinking:	**Teacher thinking:**
Saying: • *I can divide it in half and then split it in half again.* • *Do you think this is about half?* • *You can put these two parts together to make $\frac{1}{4}$ and these two parts together to make $\frac{1}{4}$.*	*Noticing:* • Shows that two $\frac{1}{4}$ s can look different from one another. • Shows $\frac{1}{4}$ in several ways. • Uses reasoning to establish a half and then half again. • Puts two parts together to make a bigger part.

Doing:
- Measures each side of the squares using a ruler.
- Divides the square in half and then in half again by estimating half and then drawing a line.
- Orally labels each region as $\frac{1}{4}$ or combines two regions to make $\frac{1}{4}$.
- Uses a design to show $\frac{1}{4}$ when $\frac{1}{4}$ is separated into two $\frac{1}{8}$s.

Representing:

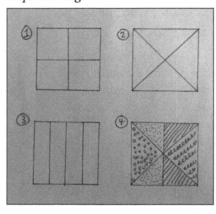

Interpreting:
- Reasons that $\frac{1}{4}$ is half of a half.
- Reasons that $\frac{1}{4}$ is two $\frac{1}{8}$s.
- Understands two equivalent fractions of a region can look different from each other.

Confirming:
- *What did you do?*
- *How did you know that each piece is exactly $\frac{1}{4}$?*
- *How might you convince someone that all $\frac{1}{4}$s have the same area?*
- *How did you know which sections to combine to make $\frac{1}{4}$?*

Responding:
- *What would it sound like to count by $\frac{1}{4}$s?*
- *When might it be useful to count that way?*
- *What other fractions would be easy to show now that you have made these? How would you do it?*
- *How do you know for sure that each section has the same area?*

Grade 3–5 Learning Experience #2

Learning Intentions: To show that the same quantity can describe many different situations.

Success Criteria:

Students will
- establish the quantity of a regional part using a strategy that makes sense for the situation
- relate the numerator to the total number of unit fractions
- compare a fractional part to the whole

What I know about my learner	What I want my learner to know
• Arranges objects efficiently to find quantities, including grouping, to allow for multiplication. • Uses schema and visualization to estimate quantities for two-digit and some smaller three-digit numbers. • Relates common fractions to decimals in familiar contexts (e.g., money). • Partitions to create fractions of a region with 2-D shapes. • Understands that the digit 2 in the number 123 has a value of 20. • Decomposes numbers in a variety of ways to solve addition and subtraction problems.	• Break an array into parts that will allow for the use of known facts to solve multiplication problems. • Modify estimations as new information becomes available. • Explain why the whole matters when talking about fractions. • Use fractions to describe sets. • Explore the symmetry on a place value chart and make connections between whole and decimal numbers. • Critically assess the situation to determine the advantages and disadvantages of different strategies used for addition and subtraction.

Learning Experience
When is $\frac{3}{4}$ a lot? When is it a little?

Student thinking:	Teacher thinking:
Saying: • *Three-quarters of something is almost the whole thing.* • *I need to think of things that are big and compare them to something that is small.* • *The summer break goes so fast; the school year goes so slow.* *Doing:* • Uses hand and arm gestures. • Looks around the classroom.	*Noticing:* • Understands that $\frac{3}{4}$ of something big is a lot, and $\frac{3}{4}$ of something small is a little. • Understands that $\frac{3}{4}$ can describe different things. • Uses gestures to help communicate the size of objects. *Interpreting:* • Uses a fraction to describe measurements including mass, area, and time. • Knows that $\frac{3}{4}$ is almost a whole but not quite. • Communicates in a variety of both verbal and non-verbal ways to project meaning.

Representing:	Confirming:
¾ of a Jolly rancher is little and ¾ of a pizza is allot ¾ of a cookie is little ¾ of a soccer stadium is allot ¾ of a school year is allot ¾ of summer break is little ¾ of a school is allot ¾ of a classroom is little	• How did you decide if something was a lot or a little? • How does looking at the fraction $\frac{3}{4}$ tell you that it is almost a whole but not quite? • How might you convince someone that you are right for each situation? *Responding:* • In what situations could you consider $\frac{3}{4}$ of a cookie a lot? • How does knowing you have $\frac{3}{4}$ of something helpful? • Is it more important to know the fraction or to know the whole when you are talking about dividing something? Why?

Additional Learning Experiences to Support Learning Quantity

- When is it useful to know that $\frac{4}{8}$ is the same as $\frac{1}{2}$?
- Choose an interesting fraction. Model your fraction in different ways. What does each way tell about the fraction?
- Suppose you know the perimeter of a rectangle is 24 cm. What other rectangles would you know the perimeters of?
- The sum of two numbers is about triple the difference. What could the numbers be?

Grade 6–10 Learner Experience #1

Learning Intentions: To estimate capacity.

Success Criteria:

Students will

- make a good judgment in a measurement situation
- decide whether an estimate is a good enough description of a measurement situation
- compare two figures in terms of different measurements

What I know about my learner	What I want my learner to know
<ul><li>Compares two shapes in terms of one measurement.</li><li>Compares the measurement of two shapes or figures that are very different.</li><li>Estimates when using whole number measurements.</li><li>Determines the circumference of a circle.</li><li>Determines the area of various shapes.</li><li>Measures and estimates using direct approaches.</li><li>Describes capacity and volume.</li><li>Describes circumference.</li><li>Describes the relationship between radius and diameter.</li></ul>	<ul><li>Compare two figures in terms of different measurements.</li><li>Compare the measurement of two figures that are not very different.</li><li>Estimate using measurements that are not whole numbers.</li><li>Decide whether an estimate is a good enough description of a measurement situation.</li><li>Understand the relationship between the area of a base and height and the volume of a figure.</li><li>Develop, interpret, and apply volume formulas and use knowledge of formulas to relate measurements.</li><li>Develop and apply procedures to calculate the volume of figures.</li></ul>

Learning Experience

Which holds more? What makes you say that?

Figure 1   Figure 2

Student thinking:	Teacher thinking:
Saying: • *Figure 2 is a lot taller.* • *Figure 1 is a lot shorter.* • *Even though Figure 1 is almost twice as wide, Figure 2 is like three times taller.*	*Noticing:* • Uses direct procedures to measure. • Makes an estimate using standard units. • Relies on past experience to support thinking.

- *Because it is taller than wider, I think Figure 2 holds more, but I am not sure because Figure 1 is wider and I can fit more popcorn on top.*

Doing:
- Uses a ruler to measure the diameter of each of the figures.
- Uses a ruler to measure the height of each figure.

Representing:

Interpreting:
- Compares the two figures using the measurements of diameter and the height.
- Applies understanding of the relationship between the area of a base and height and the volume of a figure.
- Distinguishes between volume and capacity.

Confirming:
- *What measurements helped you estimate?*
- *What is the difference between volume and capacity?*
- *How have you determined the volume of a figure before?*

Responding:
- *How might you confirm your estimate?*
- *How might the area of the base help you?*
- *What might you do to the shapes to make the capacity very different?*

Grade 6–10 Learning Experience #2

Learning Intentions: To estimate.

Success Criteria:

Students will
- identify what they know and what they need to know
- make a good judgment in an estimation situation
- decide whether or not an estimate is reasonable

What I know about my learner	What I want my learner to know
• Estimates when using whole number measurements. • Solves problems using additive thinking. • Solves problems using addition and subtraction. • Uses additive relationships to compare quantities.	• Decide whether an estimate is a good enough description of a measurement situation. • Solve proportional reasoning problems. • Use multiplicative relationships to compare quantities.

- Compares quantities or values.
- Uses numbers up to 1,000 in context.
- Identifies patterns in the number system involving whole numbers.

- Use partial measurements to make predictions.
- Use numbers into the 1,000,000s in context.

Learning Experience

How many birds might there be in this tree? Explain your thinking.

Student thinking:	Teacher thinking:

Saying:
• I think there are about 20 birds on each branch.
• I am guessing there are about 10 branches on half the tree.
• Then I doubled to figure out how many are on the whole tree.
 	
Doing:
• Counts the number of birds on one branch.
• Counts the number of branches on half the tree.
 	
Representing:
 	
20+20+20+20+20
    +20 +20 +20 +20 +20
        = 100 + 100
        = 200
 	
200+200 = 400
	Noticing:
	• Counts the number of birds on one branch of the tree.
	• Estimates the number of branches on the whole tree.
	
	Interpreting:
	• Uses one-to-one correspondence when counting the numbers of birds on the tree.
	• Uses one-to-one correspondence when counting the number of branches on half the tree.
	• Uses additive thinking to determine the number of birds on half of the tree.
	• Uses multiplicative thinking (i.e., doubling) to determine the number of birds in the tree.

Confirming:

- *What do you know?*
- *How did the number of branches help you?*
- *What strategy did you use to determine the number of birds on half the tree? The whole tree?*

Responding:

- *How else might you have solved this problem?*
- *How does your strategy compare to your partner's?*
- *What would happen to the number of birds if the height of the tree doubled?*

Additional Learning Experiences to Support Learning Quantity

- What fraction is a little more than $\frac{3}{4}$ and less than 1?
- How do you know that $\frac{3}{4}$ of $\frac{2}{3}$ is less than the sum of $\frac{3}{4}$ and $\frac{2}{3}$ without making any calculations?
- When would x^3 be less than x^2?
- The solution to an equation is $n = -4$. What might the equation be?
- One solution to a quadratic equation is $n = 2$. What might the equation be?

Counting

Stella started full-day kindergarten in September and is enjoying being immersed in French in the rich play-based learning environment. Her educators, Sara and Micheline, are co-creating with the students as they explore wonderings and rely on thinking skills to promote literacy and mathematics. Throughout the day, Stella is encouraged to read, write, count, quantify, and subitize the world around her. The classroom is a free-flowing space where children, educators, and materials migrate to where the learning is happening. Today, Stella is engaging with learning at the dramatic play centre, a pizzeria, fitted with a co-constructed counter, pizza oven, menus, and a sign adorned with hand-painted letters, "Perfct Pizza Plase." Stella is preparing materials for a large party of her classmates, which requires forks, knives, plates, and cups, "Just like a real pizzeria." Stella rhymes off numbers as she counts the forks, "1, 2, 3, 4, 5, 7, 8, 9, 10." There are 7 forks. After hearing her classmate counting in French, she counts the knives, "Un, deux, trois, quatre, cinq, sept, huit, neuf, dix." There are 6 knives. What ensues is a lovely debate between Stella and her buddy, Sophie. Sophie prompts Stella, "It goes 1, 2, 3, 4, 5, 6, 7, 8, 9, 10." Sophie emphasizes the 6 by saying this number slower and louder than the others. Stella retorts, "No, it goes 1, 2, 3, 4, 5, 7, 8, 9, 10!" Back and forth, the students engage in a spirited debate, Sophie trying, in her five-year old way, several different approaches to convince Stella that she is missing the number 6 in both languages. No small feat. Sara, the educator, carefully observes and decides to allow Sophie the space to help Stella construct the counting order. After Sophie's valiant attempts are exhausted, the educator quietly steps in and asks, "Stella, count 6 forks." Stella responds, "1, 2, 3, 4, 5, 6." "How about trying in French?" Stella rhymes off the numbers, "un, deux, trois, quatre, cinq, six!"

This subtle intervention by the educator in a natural counting situation demonstrates a proficient understanding of both the principles of counting and the development of counting. Sara understands that Stella has established a stable order for counting, but also identifies that Stella's stable order excludes "6," preventing her from using the conventional order for numbers. Sara wants Stella to acknowledge

"6," and she knows the best way to do this is have Stella count to 6. Furthermore, she also knows that she needs Stella to generalize that 6 follows 5 in other situations, not just when you are counting to 6. Knowing this, Sara continues the conversation in hopes Stella will start to generalize the conventional counting order:

> Sara: "Stella, what did you notice about the number 6 when you were counting to 6?"
>
> Stella: After thoughtful reflection, she responds by sharing, "6 comes after 5."
>
> Sara: "Do you think that it makes sense that 6 should come after 5 when you are counting to other numbers?"
>
> Stella: "I think so." Then, turns to Sophie, "Will you help me count the knives and forks again?"
>
> Sophie: "Let's do this!"

THE IMPORTANT STUFF

- The counting principles help us to count with meaning.
- Counting strategies are useful when performing operations with numbers.
- Counting tells us how many are in a set.

Counting Principles:

- There is one and only one number said for each object (One-to-One Principle).
- There is a consistent set of counting words that never changes (Stable Order Principle).
- The last number spoken tells how many (Cardinal Principle).
- It does not matter what you count; the process for counting remains the same (Abstraction Principle).
- It does not matter in which order you count; the number in the set does not change (Order Relevance Principle).

(Gelman & Gallistel, 1978)

Making Sense of Counting

Students' early understanding of the five principles of counting is among the earliest ways that students start to gain understanding of the number system. Counting starts at a very early age. Children's pre-counting starts at around 1 year of age when they begin to experiment by saying random numbers in no particular order. As children continue to incrementally develop a more sophisticated understanding of counting over time, they eventually come to understand some important number concepts:

- You can count forwards or backwards.
- Numbers can be conserved, allowing for counting on.
- There are patterns in the number system that can be perpetually applied when counting.

- The same set of objects can be identified and counted by using two numbers: one set of 10 objects can be described as **one** set allowing the set to be skip-counted by tens, and it can also be described as **10** objects allowing the same set to be counted by ones.

The phenomenon that sets can be represented using two different numbers is sometimes called unitizing. This understanding is fundamental as students transition from additive to multiplicative thinking and allows students to use skip counting as a strategy for multiplying in some contexts. Conversely, skip counting backwards can be used as a strategy for division in other situations. Understanding the small steps between pre-counting strategies to the sophistication of unitizing allows us to notice, interpret, and respond to the learner in our classrooms.

Counting in Many Contexts

It is generally accepted that counting large collections is more challenging and sophisticated than counting small collections. Furthermore, counting by numbers other than one, including larger whole numbers and smaller fractional parts, increases the challenge and effort initially, while these skills become more automatic over time. However, there are other ways to offer students increasingly challenging opportunities for counting. For example:

- *Size*: Students develop the principles of counting with smaller collections first and begin to generalize the principles in these situations. Later, they apply the same principles to larger sets.
- *Arrangement:* Objects arranged in a row are most approachable for students. The starting and ending place are pre-established and do not require tracking by the young counter. Objects arranged in circular arrangements force students to track and hold the starting and ending place while they count. Randomly placed objects push their ability to track and hold the objects that have and have not been counted.
- *Fixed versus moveable:* A collection such as loose counters will allow students to move or slide the object as they count and clearly separate the objects that are counted from those that are yet to be counted. A collection that is fixed (e.g., counting objects on a picture) does not provide the same opportunity and requires more mental tracking.

Opportunity for Reflection

What opportunities are you giving your students to count? Are the opportunities increasingly sophisticated?

Using Prompting to Think About Counting

Consider how the thinking stems and prompting questions identified on the following page can be applied to a wide range of counting opportunities across different math strands.

Thinking stems:

I counted by . . . because . . .
I know there are . . . because . . .
I organized this collection by . . . because . . .
I keep track by . . .
I find it easy to count when . . .
I find it harder to count when . . .
If I can count to . . . I know I can also count to . . . because . . .

Prompting questions:

How might you organize . . . to help you count?
Why does counting by . . . make sense in this situation?
I see you chose to count by . . . What other ways might make sense? Not make sense?
What might happen if . . .?
How did you keep track of the objects you have already counted?
How are counting and adding/subtraction/multiplication/division the same? How are they different?
I noticed you . . . when you counted. Why does that make sense?

How Will We Know Our Students Understand Counting?

We will know that our students understand counting when we hear or see them doing the following:

☐ Touching one object and saying one number for each object that they count.

☐ Consistently using the conventional counting order, including counting by parts of numbers (e.g., fractions or decimals) and skip counting.

☐ Understanding that the last number said when counting represents the quantity in the set.

☐ Considering the situation and deciding on a counting strategy that fits the situation.

☐ Organizing the collection in a way that makes it easy to count, including combining parts of wholes to make wholes (e.g., combining two halves to make a whole).

☐ Conserving a portion of the collection being counted and finding the total by counting on.

Opportunity for Reflection

How might you count this collection? What opportunities does this task provide students to demonstrate their understanding of counting?

The progression shown in Figure 4.1 demonstrates a simplified version of how children develop counting skills over time as they move from foundational understandings to more sophisticated understandings. It is possible and likely that students will be working in more than one phase at a time. Although synthesized from research, this progression is an approximation of how students might develop over time and is not intended to be a fulsome picture.

- Rote counts to 20.
- Counts and creates small collections.
- Recognizes errors in others' counting.

- Skip counts by 2s, 5s, and 10s to 100.
- Counts on by ones.
- Counts backwards from 20.
- Counts through the decade numbers.

- Skip counts by 2s, 5s, and 10s through 100.
- Skip counts backwards by 2s, 5s, and 10s from 100 starting from a multiple of 2, 5, or 10.
- Counts mental images of hidden objects.

- Combines parts to make wholes to count.
- Counts different ways to larger numbers.
- Counts collections of money efficiently.
- Uses skip counting to solve multiplication and division problems.

Figure 4.1: Sample Progression for Counting

(Adapted from Small, 2005; Clements & Sarama, 2014)

Learning Experiences

The following learning experiences are organized into grade bands: Kindergarten–Grade 2, Grade 3–5, and Grade 6–10. They are designed to demonstrate how you can use your students as resources to plan for and deliver responsive tasks based on a sample progression of learning. We have used learning experiences from across the strands of mathematics to help key number ideas emerge.

Kindergarten–Grade 2 Learning Experience #1

Learning Intentions: To organize objects to make it easier to count.

Success Criteria:

Students will

- organize a collection of objects to make it easy to count
- use what they know about one collection to count another collection
- track the objects that have already been counted

What I know about my learner	What I want my learner to know
<ul><li>Rhythmically counts numbers in the correct order.</li><li>Assigns one number for each object they touch but sometimes counts objects twice or not at all.</li><li>Counts each set when two sets are identical.</li><li>Recounts a set when the objects in the set are reorganized.</li><li>Counts by ones for each set.</li><li>Knows the size (magnitude) of the set is the last number said when counting.</li><li>Sorts objects by common attributes such as color and size.</li></ul>	<ul><li>Assign one number for each object in a set.</li><li>Organize the collection in a way that makes it easy to count and track.</li><li>Use information from one set to count the number in a different set.</li><li>Understand the total number of objects remains the same unless some are added or taken away.</li><li>Know there are lots of ways to count and some ways are more efficient than others in certain situations.</li><li>Know that two numbers can describe the same set: a set of 10 objects can be described as one set of 10 objects or 10 objects.</li></ul>

Learning Experience

You start sorting classroom objects by putting these two objects together:

Tell what the sorting rule might be. Then, find other objects from the classroom that go with these ones. Tell how many are in the group.

Student thinking:	Teacher thinking:
Saying: • *They are both orange.* • *A juice box is orange.* • *1, 2, 3, 4, 5, 6, 7, 8! There are 8 objects.* *Doing:* • Does a 360 degree scan of the room. • Gathers objects from around the classroom, including a pencil, blocks, and a juice box, and adds them to a pile with the marker and ball. *Representing:* • Places objects in a pile on the carpet in the classroom.	*Noticing:* • Uses conventional counting order. • Touches an object for each word said in the counting sequence. • Touches the juice box twice. • Confirms there are eight objects in the pile after counting. *Interpreting:* • Uses a stable order when counting objects. • Uses synchrony and one-to-one tagging by touching and saying a word for each object but does not track the items already touched. • Counts the objects again when they are moved. • Might still think that the number of objects has changed if they count twice and get two different numbers. *Confirming:* • *Tell me about your sorting rule.* • *Can you tell me about how you counted?* • *(Move objects intentionally.) How many objects are now in the pile?* *Responding:* • *How might you organize the objects to make it easier to count?*

- *What would happen if I added one more object?*
- (Add a second column of objects matching right beside each other.) *What do you notice about the size of these two columns? How might that help you to know how many are in this group?*

Kindergarten–Grade 2 Learning Experience #2

Learning Intentions: To group numbers to make it easier to count.

Success Criteria:

Students will
- understand that a collection can be described using different numbers, the total number of objects, and/or the number of groups
- organize objects in a way that makes it easy to count and explain their choice
- match a counting strategy to the situation

What I know about my learner	What I want my learner to know
<ul><li>Assigns one number for each object in a set.</li><li>Organizes a collection of objects in a row to make it easy to count.</li><li>Moves counted objects to a "counted" pile after counting.</li><li>Uses information from one set to count the number in a different set.</li><li>Understands that the total number of objects remains the same unless some are added or taken away.</li><li>Skip counts by 2s to 20 and by 5s to 30 rhythmically.</li></ul>	<ul><li>Group objects to skip count.</li><li>Know there are lots of ways to count and some ways are more efficient than others in certain situations.</li><li>Know that two numbers can describe the same set: a set of 10 objects can be described as one set of 10 objects or 10 objects.</li><li>Skip count in context by 2s, 5s, and 10s to 100.</li><li>Use a combination of skip counting and counting on by ones when there are unequal groups.</li></ul>

Learning Experience
Shane makes a repeating shape pattern in a way that makes it easy to count the number of shapes quickly. What might Shane's pattern look like? How might he have counted?

Student thinking:	Teacher thinking:
Saying: • *My pattern rule is triangle, triangle, circle, circle, circle.* • *5, 10, 15, 20, 25 . . . there are 25!* • *1, 2, 3, 4, 5, 6, 7, . . . , 23, 24, 25.* *Doing:* • Points to shapes with finger and mouths a word starting with the first shape; repeats several times while creating the pattern. • Shows the pattern to a friend when done. • Uses fingers to form a frame around the first five elements when showing the pattern to a friend. *Representing:* 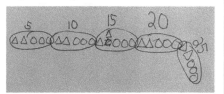	*Noticing:* • Counts by 5s and then by 1s. • Corrects an error in the pattern by replacing a circle with a triangle. • Creates a pattern core with five elements. • Circles groups of five elements and adds the number said when counting. *Interpreting:* • Not yet confident with skip counting and wants to double-check by counting by ones. • Has a system for tracking the accuracy of a pattern that includes starting at the beginning and saying the pattern while touching the elements of the pattern. • Creates a pattern with five elements because that is a number they are comfortable counting by. *Confirming:* • *Why did you count by both 5s and 1s?* • *How did you know you made a mistake?* • *How did you decide what pattern rule you should use?* *Responding:* • *How many objects are there? How many groups are there? How can this pattern have 5 and 25?* • *How might you count if someone added seven more shapes to your pattern?* • *How else might someone count this collection other than by 1s or 5s?*

- Kristina says the number 17 while counting something in the classroom but she does not start counting at 1. What might she be counting? How might she have counted?
- *(Provide a collection of common 2-D shapes.)* Choose a sorting rule that works for these shapes. Organize the shapes in a way that makes it hard to count how many are in each pile. Then, sort the shapes in a way that makes it easy to count how many are in each pile.
- Create a picture with 2-D shapes. Count the total number of sides of all the shapes. Tell how you know you are right.
- How can you skip count and say the number 37? Tell the number you started with and how much you skipped each time.
- A collection of counters is organized in a way that makes it hard to count. What might the collection look like? How would you organize the collection to make it easier to count?
- You count a collection of objects and say 12 when you are almost done counting. What collection might you have counted?
- You are counting the sides on two-dimensional shapes and you decide to skip count. What shapes might you be using? Why does skip counting make sense?

Grade 3–5 Learning Experience #1

Learning Intentions: To link skip counting to addition, subtraction, multiplication, and division.

Success Criteria:

Students will
- create an area model and link it to skip counting
- describe skip counting using a number sentence
- reflect on the similarities and differences between counting and operations

What I know about my learner	What I want my learner to know
<ul><li>Arranges objects into groups to make it easy to count.</li><li>Chooses a counting strategy that fits the situation.</li><li>Knows that two numbers can describe the same set: a set of 10 objects can be described as one set of 10 objects or 10 objects.</li><li>Skip counts in context by 2s, 5s, and 10s to 100.</li><li>Uses a combination of skip counting and counting on by ones when there are unequal groups.</li></ul>	<ul><li>Arrange groups of objects into arrays.</li><li>Justify choice of counting strategy and defend why it is a good strategy for the situation.</li><li>Combine fractional parts to make wholes to make it easier to count.</li><li>Count money by counting larger valued coins and grouping smaller valued coins.</li><li>Connect skip counting forwards to multiplication and skip</li></ul>

• Finds the area of a rectangle by creating a rectangle on grid paper or with tiles and counting the tiles.	counting backwards to division to help solve problems.

Learning Experience

You notice someone skip counting to find the area of a rectangle on grid paper. What might the rectangle look like? Think of lots of possibilities.

Student thinking:	**Teacher thinking:**
Saying: • *They probably counted by 2s, 5s, or 10s so I think we should make rectangles with one of the side lengths that long.* • *2, 4, 6, . . . 22* • *Look, we could count half and then double it.* *Doing:* • Draws a dot on the vertex of a square on the paper and touches each of the vertices directly below it while appearing to count. • Draws a vertical line from the top dot to the bottom dot. • Draws two matching horizontal lines from the top and bottom dots. • Connects the horizontal lines at the other end. 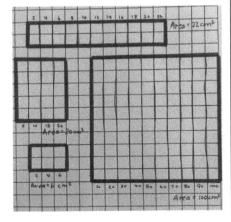	*Noticing:* • Counts by 2s, 5s, and 10s. • Labels the drawing with numbers. • Touches each column in the rectangle and says one number for each touch. • Makes a connection to addition. *Interpreting:* • Proficiently counts by 2s, 5s, and 10s and believes that others can do the same. • Adds numbers and writing to the representation to make thinking visible to others. • Looks for connections and efficient ways to solve for the area of a rectangle. • Understands the connection between skip counting and addition. *Confirming:* • *How did you decide what the rectangles should look like?* • *Why did you represent your thinking this way?* • *Would you use skip counting to find the area of these rectangles? Why?* • *How is skip counting like adding? How is it different?*

Responding:
- *When is skip counting a good strategy to find the area of a rectangle? When is it not such a good strategy?*
- *How could you show your counting strategy with an equation?*
- *Could you use a different operation in your number sentence?*
- *Is skip counting more like adding or more like multiplication? Why?*

Grade 3–5 Learning Experience #2

Learning Intentions: To combine parts to make wholes to help count.

Success Criteria:

Students will
- adapt known counting strategies to count fractional parts
- make connections between situations when counting fractions
- describe why counting strategies are effective for a situation

What I know about my learner	What I want my learner to know
- Arranges objects into groups to make it easy to count. - Chooses a counting strategy that fits the situation. - Knows that two numbers can describe the same set: a set of 10 objects can be described as one set of 10 objects or 10 objects. - Skip counts in context by 2s, 5s, and 10s and fractions by $\frac{1}{4}$ and $\frac{1}{2}$. - Uses a combination of skip counting and counting on by ones when there are unequal groups. - Arranges groups of objects into arrays. - Knows many common number facts.	- Justify choice of counting strategy and defend why it is a good strategy for the situation. - Combine fractional parts to make wholes to make it easier to count. - Count money by counting larger valued coins and grouping smaller valued coins. - Connect counting money to counting fractions. - Connect skip counting forwards to multiplication and skip counting backwards to division to help solve problems.

↓

Learning Experience

Count the dots that you see. Explain how you know you are right.

Student thinking:	Teacher thinking:
Saying: • *I multiplied the big section first then took away the missing parts.* • *I grouped the smaller parts together to make wholes, two halves to make a whole, and two quarters and a half to make a whole.* *Doing:* • Studies the picture for a while before starting. • Draws small circles in the air while studying the picture. *Representing:* 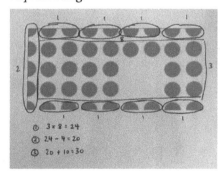	*Noticing:* • Uses the words counting, addition, and multiplication to talk about their strategy. • Deals with the wholes separately from the parts. • Outlines a 3 × 8 array. • Groups two halves to make a whole and three halves and two quarters to make two wholes. *Interpreting:* • Uses a flexible approach to counting. • Is more comfortable working with wholes than fractional parts. • Creates arrays that match known facts. • Counts flexibly between quarters and halves to make wholes. *Confirming:* • *What did you do? Why?* • *Why did you choose to group the dots the way that you did?* • *How did you use counting to help you determine the number of dots?*

	Responding: • *What advice would you give someone who was trying to count a collection with a mix of wholes and parts?* • *How is counting these dots like counting money? How are they different?*

Additional Learning Experiences to Support Learning Counting

- Choose one of these expressions:

  5×7 8×10 9×2

  Tell how you could use skip counting to find the product.
- Ali is skip counting by 2s. Aarya is skip counting by 5s. What number would each of them have to start at to get to 100 at about the same time?
- When might you say the number 2 ½ when counting?
- In what situations would it make sense to skip count to solve a division problem? In what situations would it not make sense?
- Zia says she knows how to count by 10s starting from 11 because she knows how to count by 10s starting from 10. Does that make sense to you?

Grade 6–10 Learner Experience #1

Learning Intentions: To compare patterns.

Success Criteria:

Students will
- use stated evidence to draw conclusions
- identify the constant in a linear growing pattern
- identify the multiplier in a linear growing pattern
- justify their thinking by reasoning with evidence

What I know about my learner	What I want my learner to know
• Identifies and extends simple patterns. • Identifies errors in the extension of simple patterns. • Creates simple patterns. • Describes simple patterns. • Determines missing terms from simple patterns. • Writes pattern rules for simple patterns.	• Identify and extend more complex non-repeating patterns. • Justify complex pattern extensions. • Represent pattern rules using math language. • Identify linear relationships. • Make predictions about growing patterns. • Write pattern rules for complex non-repeating patterns.

Learning Experience

How are these patterns alike? How are they different?

Pattern 1

Pattern 2

Student thinking:	Teacher thinking:
Saying: • *Both are getting bigger.* • *Both are growing patterns, but they are growing by different amounts.* • *They start at different amounts.* *Doing:* • Circles three dots in each term for pattern 1. • Circles one dot in each term for pattern 2. • Counts remaining dots for each term for both patterns. *Representing:*	*Noticing:* • Circles the same number of dots in pattern 1 to identify the constant. • Circles the same number of dots in pattern 2 to identify the constant. • Identifies the remaining dots for each pattern to determine the multiplier. *Interpreting:* • Recognizes that the pattern has a constant and a multiplier that could be used to determine a general rule for each pattern. • Recognizes that each pattern is a linear growing pattern. *Confirming:* • *What is happening in the pattern?* • *What kind of pattern is it? How do you know?* • *How is the pattern growing?* • *How did you make the decision to circle three dots in pattern 1?*

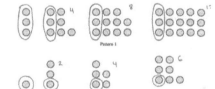

Alike
- both have 4 terms
- both go up by an even number
- both are growing patterns
- both go up by the same amount each time
- both have constants
- both have multipliers

Different
- pattern 1 is growing more
- both start at different numbers
- pattern 1 went up by 4 each time
- pattern 2 goes up by 2 each time
- if I graphed them they would look different

Responding:
- *What might the graphical representations look like?*
- *What are the pattern rules for each pattern?*
- *If you circled only one dot in pattern 1, how would that change the pattern rule?*
- *How might you determine what the 30th term looks like?*

Grade 6–10 Learning Experience #2

Learning Intentions: To find the perimeter of composite shapes.

Success Criteria:

Students will
- describe perimeter
- use non-standard units to determine the perimeter
- develop a strategy to determine the perimeter
- describe composite shapes

What I know about my learner	What I want my learner to know
• Determines the perimeter of simple figures given the dimensions. • Determines the perimeter of simple figures by measuring the length. • Describes perimeter as the sum of the side lengths. • Recognizes that two shapes can have the same area even though the perimeters are different. • Constructs simple shapes (e.g., rectangles, squares, triangles) given the perimeter using standard and non-standard units.	• Determine the perimeter of composite shapes. • Use measurement shortcuts to solve problems. • Construct composite shapes given the perimeter.

↓

Learning Experience

Which shapes have a perimeter of less than 20?

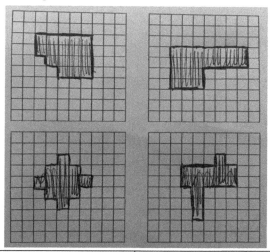

Student thinking:	Teacher thinking:
Saying: • *I know I have to find the total distance around the shape.* • *The grid will help me because each square on the grid has a length of one unit.* *Doing:* • Places a dash on every non-standard unit of one. • Counts all the dashes to determine to the total perimeter. *Representing:*	*Noticing:* • Represents each non-standard unit of one with a dash. • Begins at one dash and counts the number of dashes around the entire shape. *Interpreting:* • Recognizes that perimeter represent the distance around the shape. *Confirming:* • *What strategy did you use?* • *How did you decide on the strategy?* • *What makes these shapes different from the others you have explored?* *Responding:* • *Which figure has the greatest area?* • *What might another shape look like?* • *Which strategy would you use to create your own shape?*

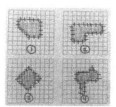

Figure	Perimeter
1	18
2	22
3	20
4	22

Additional Learning Experiences to Support Learning Counting

- Draw a shape on a 100 grid that has a perimeter of less than 30 units.
- Estimate the area of the shape.

Relating

Derek observes his class as they are experimenting with angles and takes strategic positions throughout the room to listen in on the learning that is happening. Today, he has challenged his students to create several triangles that look a lot different from each other and measure the internal angles. His teaching philosophy is to try not to step in front of the struggle and instead to stand by and guide students to construct his learning goals. Aarya is working hard with her protractor to measure the angles of an acute triangle while her partner looks on. She measures one of the acute angles on her triangle and announces, "113°!" Her partner, Aleena, quickly jumps in, "I don't think that is right, see, the angle is an acute angle, so it has to measure less than 90°." Aleena adds reasoning to her argument, "It is about half way between a half-right angle and a right angle, so it should be between about 65° and 70°." Aarya grabs her protractor and proceeds to measure the angle one more time. A look of realization crosses her face. She had inadvertently read the protractor from the wrong side. "63°," she says.

Derek does not want this moment to pass without Aarya articulating the importance of what has just happened:

Derek: "Aarya, what advice might you give someone who is learning to measure angles?"

Aarya: "Make sure you read the protractor from the right side!"

Derek: "That does sound important. How might a mathematician know if they have read a protractor from the wrong side, by accident?"

Aarya: (A short pause) "Well … they should probably think about the angle first. Like Aleena, she used angles that she knows, like a right angle and a half-right angle, and estimated the angle."

Derek: "Let's try that. Estimate the angles on your triangles and convince Aleena your estimates make sense."

Making Sense of Relating

The concept of relating is closely tied to students' development of quantity and counting. With the development of counting and quantity, students begin to compare and relate numbers to each other. Some of the very earliest experiences with relating numbers begin with students' exploration of *more* and *less*. They intrinsically begin this process early in their life and start to understand these concepts through real-life contexts (e.g., "She got more than me."). As students begin to develop counting and quantity concepts over time, their ability to relate quantities also becomes more sophisticated. For example, in the early stages, a student who counts a collection of five big blocks and then counts a collection of five small blocks might not yet be able to compare the two groups to determine that the two groups have the same amount. Later, the student might place two objects on a 10-frame to help quickly determine which has more. Still later, the same student might line up two collections to quickly determine how many more are in the bigger group. Over time, these incremental steps in understanding will lead to understanding that benchmarks are helpful for making sense of a number and that the same number can represent a big amount in some situations and a small amount in a different situation (e.g., $100 is a lot to pay for a chocolate bar; $100 is a little to pay for a new car).

You can help students develop an understanding of benchmark numbers over time in many contexts across the strands of math. It is helpful to introduce mathematical models that will help students develop this skill. In the early years, students might compare a number to a benchmark of 10 by using a 10-frame or compare the length of something to their height by creating a string model of their height. Later, they might compare six-digit numbers to 1,000,000 on an open number line or compare angles to a right or straight angle by modeling each benchmark angle.

Making Generalizations

One of our goals as teachers is to carefully introduce our students to mathematical situations that will help them to develop deep conceptual understandings. As students develop sophisticated strategies and big ideas, we want to help students see the connections between what they are currently exploring and their previous experiences, and we want to help them formalize the relationships that are inherent in the number system. When students are constructing concepts, they make conjectures about mathematical situations but often require educator intervention to test and formalize a generalization about a mathematical relationship. At each step of the way, it is helpful to have a bank of prompts that will help make these relationships visible. Figure 6.1 outlines the process students follow to make generalizations, as well as sample prompts teachers can use during this process.

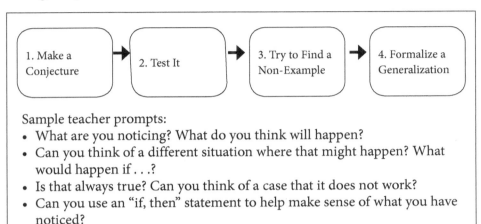

Sample teacher prompts:
- What are you noticing? What do you think will happen?
- Can you think of a different situation where that might happen? What would happen if . . .?
- Is that always true? Can you think of a case that it does not work?
- Can you use an "if, then" statement to help make sense of what you have noticed?

Figure 5.1: Making Generalizations

Relating Parts of the Four Operations

As students develop the four operations over time, they come to understand how the parts of a number sentence relate to each other. As they move through a progression for operational sense, we can help students formalize these relationships by supporting the making of generalizations. It can be helpful for students to name the different parts of each operation, although it should be recognized that it is much more important for students to understand how the parts relate to each other than to know what each part of an equation is called (see Figure 5.2).

Addition	Subtraction
2 + 3 = 5 Addend Addend Sum or Total	6 – 1 = 5 Minuend Subtrahend Difference
Multiplication	**Division**
6 × 3 = 18 Factor Factor Product (or Multiplier) (or Multiplicand)	10 ÷ 2 = 5 Dividend Divisor Quotient

Figure 5.2: The Parts of Each Operation

Researchers have demonstrated the importance of students using known facts to find unknown facts, often called derived facts. Many derived fact strategies appear early and progress with increasing sophistication over time (Dowker, 2013). The ability to use known facts to solve unknown facts makes students more efficient mathematicians by enabling them to quickly adapt knowledge to new situations. All efficient mental math strategies for solving operations rely on students having a bank of known facts; therefore, automaticity of some facts is important. Students should have many opportunities to develop fluency of math facts in a safe, anxiety-free learning environment with an emphasis on developing number sense over rote memorization of the facts (Boaler, 2015) (see Figure 5.3).

STRATEGIES TO DEVELOP NUMBER SENSE

Addition

Generalization	Sample Learning Experience
If I add 1 to an addend and the other remains the same, then I add 1 to the sum.	*How does knowing 5 + 5 = 10 help you to solve 5 + 6?*
If I subtract 1 from an addend and the other remains the same, then I subtract 1 from the sum.	10 + 10 10 + 9 5 + 5 4 + 5 20 + 20 20 + 19
If I move 1 from the first addend to the second addend, then the sum remains the same.	*What is the sum of 91 + 89?*
If I add 1 to an addend and subtract 1 later, then the sum remains the same.	Noah adds two numbers together by changing each addend a little bit and fixing it up later. What two numbers might he have added? How might he have added them?

Subtraction

Generalization	Sample Learning Experience
If I add 1 to the minuend and the subtrahend remains the same, then I add 1 to the difference.	40 – 20 41 – 20 42 – 20 52 – 20 152 – 20

If the minuend remains the same and I add 1 to the subtrahend, then I subtract 1 from the difference.	40 – 20 40 – 21 40 – 22 40 – 32
If I add the same amount to both the minuend and the subtrahend, the difference remains the same.	The difference between Harman and Simran's ages is 4. How old might they be? What will be the difference in their ages in 5, 10, 25, and 1,000 years?

Multiplication

Generalization	Sample Learning Experience
If I increase the multiplier by 1 and the multiplicand remains the same, then I add the multiplicand to the product.	4×5 4×8 5×5 5×8 6×5 6×8
If I increase the multiplicand by 1 and the multiplier remains the same, then I add the multiplier to the product.	5×4 8×4 5×5 8×5 5×6 8×6
If I double one of the factors and the other remains the same, then the product doubles.	A rectangle has an area of 24 cm². What might the length and width be? Double the length and tell what happens to the area.
If I double one of the factors and half the other factor, then the product remains the same.	8×8 4×16 2×32

Division

Generalization	Sample Learning Experience
If I double the dividend and double the divisor, then the quotient remains the same.	*How does knowing 64 ÷ 8 = 8 help you to solve 128 ÷ 16?*

If I double the dividend and the divisor remains the same, then the quotient is doubled.	How does knowing 64 ÷ 8 = 8 help you to solve 128 ÷ 8?
If the dividend remains the same and I double the divisor, then the quotient is halved.	How does knowing 64 ÷ 8 = 8 help you to solve 64 ÷ 16?

Figure 5.3

Relating Addition and Subtraction

Placing an emphasis on relating addition to subtraction helps learners become more efficient and flexible thinkers. Students tend to have a less developed number of known facts for subtraction and a less developed bank of subtraction strategies. Therefore, it is helpful for them to understand the inverse relationship between addition and subtraction so they can draw on their knowledge of addition facts and strategies to help solve subtraction problems.

Research indicates a wide range of ages at which students begin to use the inverse relationship between addition and subtraction to solve problems. Some have found that it tends not to happen until around the age of 10, while others have determined that students as young as age 7 or 8 years have been shown to use this important relationship. The discrepancy might be explained by the age at which an emphasis is placed on relating addition and subtraction in the classroom.

> "Yet it may be more difficult for children to use derived fact strategies for subtraction than addition, both because their relative lack of known facts gives them less of a base from which to use them, and because some derived fact strategies for subtraction, such as the 'subtraction by addition' strategy, depend on some understanding of the inverse relationship between addition and subtraction, which some studies suggest is difficult for children." *Dowker, 2014*

Opportunity for Reflection

Tell lots of addition and subtraction facts that this model demonstrates.

5	
2	3

What opportunities are you giving your students to relate numbers in strands other than number sense?

Relating Multiplication and Division

Similar to the development of subtraction compared to addition, there seems to be less fluency with known division facts and strategies as compared to multiplication. Because of the added complexity of developing efficiency for division, it is helpful to support students to see the inverse relationship between multiplication and division, especially in situations with more complex numbers (e.g., two-digit divisor or quotient).

Opportunity for Reflection

How might knowing how multiplication and division relate to each other help you to solve the following division problems?

$$28 \div 4 \qquad 108 \div 6 \qquad 216 \div 24$$

Using Prompting to Think About Relating

Consider how the following thinking stems and prompting questions can be applied to a wide range of counting opportunities across different math strands.

Thinking stems:

My estimate of . . . makes sense because . . .
I know this is reasonable because . . .
This model shows . . .
The relationship between . . . and . . . is . . .
I compared this number to this benchmark because . . .
What facts do you know that might help you solve this one?

Prompting questions:

When is . . . a big number? When is . . . a small number?
How does visualizing . . . help you make sense of that number?
What is a helpful benchmark in this situation?
What would happen if . . .?
What is your estimate? Why does it make sense?
If you know . . . what else do you know?
How might you describe the relationship between . . . and . . .

How Will We Know Our Students Understand Relating?

We will know that our students understand when we hear or see them doing the following:
- ☐ Making reasonable estimates and justifying their thinking using their schema.
- ☐ Showing there are lots of ways to relate two numbers to each other, some of which are additive while some are multiplicative.
- ☐ Explaining the inverse relationships between two numbers (e.g., 8 is two more than 6 and 6 is two less than 8; 8 is $\frac{1}{3}$ bigger than 6 and 6 is $\frac{1}{4}$ smaller than 8).
- ☐ Relating numbers to benchmarks to help make sense of the number.
- ☐ Using conversions in measurement to help make sense of the measurement.
- ☐ Explaining when the same number can represent something big and something small.
- ☐ "Undoing" operations by performing the opposite operation.

- ☐ Representing the same relationship in different ways interchangeably depending on the context (e.g., fractions, ratios, percent).
- ☐ Representing situations using expressions and/or equations.
- ☐ Making generalizations about operations that help make sense of the result of the operations.

Opportunity for Reflection

This is a right angle.

What other angles can you find pretty easily? What might your students say?

The progression shown in Figure 5.4 demonstrates a simplified version of how students develop a sense of relating over time as they move from foundational understandings to more sophisticated understandings. It is possible and likely that students will be working in more than one phase at a time. Although synthesized from research, this progression is an approximation of how students might develop over time and is not intended to be a fulsome picture.

- Compares two small numbers as more, less, or the same.
- Recognizes equivalence between two different arrangements of the same number.
- Compares small numbers to benchmarks of 5 and 10.

- Compares numbers to 100.
- Relates the relative size of numbers to the number of digits to compare.
- Relates common equivalent fractions.
- Compares numbers to benchmarks up to 100.
- Uses place value to compare numbers.

- Compares larger numbers.
- Compares fractions with the same denominator.
- Describes a number in terms of a unit other than 1 (e.g., 20 is ten 2s).
- Relates more complex equivalent fractions.
- Compares numbers to benchmarks up to 1,000.
- Compares decimal numbers with the same number of digits to the right of the decimal.

- Relates simple fractions to describe one fraction in terms of another.
- Understands the whole matters when comparing fractions.
- Uses multiples to relate two numbers multiplicatively.
- Relates improper fractions to one.
- Relates fractions, decimals, and percent interchangeably based on the context.

Figure 5.4: Sample Progression for Quantity

(Adapted from Small, 2005; Clements & Sarama, 2014)

Learning Experiences

The following learning experiences are organized into grade bands: Kindergarten–Grade 2, Grade 3–5, and Grade 6–10. They are designed to demonstrate how you can use your students as resources to plan for and deliver responsive tasks based on a sample progression of learning. We have used learning experiences from across the strands of mathematics to help key number ideas emerge.

Kindergarten–Grade 2 Learning Experience #1

Learning Intentions: To compare the distance between two numbers.

Success Criteria:

Students will
- relate numbers to each other using mathematical language (e.g., more, less, far)
- demonstrate that one indicator of bigger numbers is number of digits
- communicate their reasoning for comparing numbers

What I know about my learner	What I want my learner to know
<ul><li>Counts objects to determine quantity.</li><li>Knows that numbers that come later in the counting sequence are greater.</li><li>Compares groups of objects to determine if one group is more than/less than/the same as the other group.</li><li>Subitizes common arrangements to 5 and knows that a number can have more than one arrangement.</li></ul>	<ul><li>Identify one/two more or less of a number with fluency using models and strategies.</li><li>Understand there are smaller numbers inside bigger numbers.</li><li>Compare numbers additively.</li><li>Conceptually subitize larger numbers.</li><li>Notice that whole numbers greater than 10 have two or more digits and whole numbers less than 10 have one digit.</li></ul>

- Fills in a 5- or 10-frame with counters and identifies if the number is bigger or smaller than 5 or 10 respectively.
- Finds numbers under 15 on a number path either by numeral recognition or counting.

Learning Experience
Two numbers are pretty far apart on a number path. What might the numbers be? How do you know they are pretty far apart?

Student thinking:	Teacher thinking:
Saying: • *If I take a big jump, I will land here. If I take a small jump, I will land here.* • *There are lots of numbers between 1 and 10 on the floor.* *Doing:* • Goes to the floor-sized number path and walks beside it, then takes small and large jumps. • Stands on a number and talks to self while stepping on different numbers. • Points to numbers on a paper-sized number path and quietly says numbers. *Representing:* 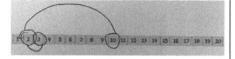	*Noticing:* • Makes big and small jumps beside or on a number path. • Notices the amount of numbers between two numbers. • Points to numbers on the number line and says numbers. *Interpreting:* • Equates "far apart" as the distance of a big jump and vice versa. • Equates "far apart" as having several numbers in between and vice versa. • Uses counting strategies to identify numbers that they do not yet recognize. *Confirming:* • *Tell me what you did.* • *How can you tell if two numbers are far apart?* • *How can you tell if two numbers are close together?* • *How might you figure out the name of a number you're not too sure about?*

	Responding: • *How many little jumps did it take to get from 2 to 3 on the number path?* • *How many little jumps did it take to get from 2 to 10 on the number path?* • (Stand on the number 10.) *How are the numbers on one side the same as the numbers on the other side? How are they different?*

Kindergarten–Grade 2 Learning Experience #2

Learning Intentions: To relate the size of the measuring unit to the measurement.

Success Criteria:

Students will

- relate that a bigger unit results in a smaller measurement
- compare two numbers and describe the relative difference between them
- use their previous experiences to make reasonable estimates and self-monitor

What I know about my learner	What I want my learner to know
• Counts objects to determine quantity. • Knows that numbers that come later in the counting sequence are greater. • Compares groups of object to determine if one group has more than/less than/the same as the other group. • Subitizes common arrangements to 5 and knows that a number can have more than one arrangement. • Fills in a 5- or 10-frame with counters and identifies if the number is bigger or smaller than 5 or 10 respectively. • Finds numbers under 15 on a number path either by numeral recognition or counting.	• Identify one/two more or less of a number with fluency using models and strategies. • Understand that there are smaller numbers inside bigger numbers. • Compare numbers additively. • Conceptually subitize larger numbers. • Notice that whole numbers greater than 10 have two or more digits and vice versa. • Understand there are many ways to measure the same object and many different units can be used to measure them.

	• Know that the bigger the unit, the smaller the measurement and vice versa.

Learning Experience

Choose something interesting in the class to measure. Tell how you could measure the object so that it sounds really big. Tell how you could measure the object so that it sounds really small.

Student thinking:	**Teacher thinking:**
Saying: • *I'm going to measure something really long.* • *1, 2, 3, . . ., 23. I measured with a paper clip.* • *It is 23 this way and 1 this way.* *Doing:* • Gathers materials for the task including paper clips and a metre stick. • Lays paperclips beside the metre stick. • Touches paper clips while silently moving lips. *Representing:* 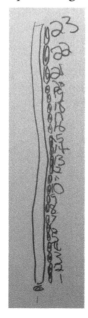	*Noticing:* • Chooses to measure a metre stick with paper clips. • Lays a metre stick on the floor and paper clips end-to-end beside its length, with a single paper clip beside its width. • Touches each paper clip and says one word for each touch. *Interpreting:* • Chooses an object that has a long dimension (length) and a short dimension (width). • Uses conventions of measurement including placing paper clips end-to-end without spaces. • Uses a counting strategy to find the linear distance for each dimension. *Confirming:* • *Tell me what you did.* • *Why did you choose to use a metre stick?* • *What advice would you give someone who is trying to measure something pretty long?* • *How do you know that your measurements are right?*

	Responding:
	• *How might you compare the numbers 1 and 23?*
	• *How is it possible for the same object to have a big measurement and a small measurement?*
	• *What do you think would happen to your measurement if you measured the length with something pretty long like your arm or pretty small like a centimetre cube?*
	• *Why do you think that happens?*

Additional Learning Experiences to Support Learning Relating

- Choose a big shape and a little shape. Measure to show that the big shape is bigger than the little shape.
- Think of a survey question you could ask where one of the answer options is a lot greater than another option. Conduct and display your survey. Compare the categories.
- One number is 10 more than another number. What could the numbers be? Think of lots of possibilities. Tell what you notice.
- A number is double a number and half of a different number. What could the numbers be? Think of lots of possibilities.

Grade 3–5 Learning Experience #1

Learning Intentions: To compare the measurements of two rectangles.

Success Criteria:

Students will
- compare measurements both additively and multiplicatively
- describe how changing the length and width of a rectangle changes the perimeter and area
- use reasoning to explain how length and width affect area

What I know about my learner	What I want my learner to know
• Compares numbers up to 100 additively. • Understands that a number can be made of several smaller parts. • Compares numbers by identifying double and half. • Uses the number of digits to help compare and relate numbers to one another.	• Compare numbers multiplicatively (e.g., 28 is 4 times more than 7). • Understand that some numbers can be divided into several equal groups. • Use digits to the right of a decimal to relate numbers to each other.

- Estimates measurements with reasoning and explains the reasoning.
- Compares numbers to landmark benchmarks (e.g., 10, 100).
- Knows there are many ways to measure the same object and that many different types of units can be used to measure.
- Understands the bigger the unit, the smaller the measurement and vice versa.
- Has developed efficient strategies for finding perimeter.
- Has developed efficient strategies for finding area.

- Make reasonable estimates and adjust estimates throughout problem solving as new information becomes available.
- Compare numbers to benchmarks using higher whole numbers in context and decimal tenths.
- Use conversions to help make sense of a measurement.
- Identify the impact on area measurements when a dimension changes.
- Compare measurements multiplicatively.

Learning Experience
Tell how you might compare the size of these two rectangles in lots of ways.

Student thinking:	Teacher thinking:
Saying: • *The white rectangle is a lot bigger than the grey rectangle.* • *Let's measure the length and the width.* • *The length and the width are both double.* • *We should use a chart.*	*Noticing:* • Uses a ruler to measure using cm. • Labels the dimensions of the rectangle. • Uses a chart. • Uses the word "double" to describe the difference between the lengths and widths.

Doing:
- Gathers a ruler and pencil.
- Places "0" on the ruler at one end of the measurement.

Representing:

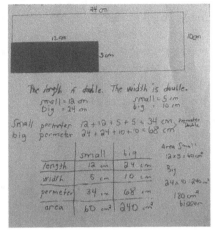

Interpreting:
- Chooses to use a suitable unit for measuring using conventions of measurement.
- Uses strategies to help make their thinking visible and organized for both themselves and others.
- Understands the relationship between double and half.

Confirming:
- *Tell me about some of the choices that you made to measure the rectangles.*
- *What did you do?*
- *Why did you choose to organize your thinking this way?*
- *I see that you used the word "double" to describe how much bigger one shape is than the other. What word describes how much shorter or slimmer the smaller one is?*

Responding:
- *How did you compare the rectangles?*
- *How is it possible for the length and width to double and the area go up a lot more?*
- *How many times could you fit the smaller rectangle inside the bigger rectangle?*
- *How might you describe that relationship using multiplication or a fraction?*

Grade 3–5 Learning Experience #2

Learning Intentions: To relate numbers to benchmarks in different ways.

Success Criteria:

Students will
- explain how a number can be relatively big and relatively small depending on the comparison
- compare two numbers additively and multiplicatively
- justify and reason how models would change if the benchmark for comparison changes

What I know about my learner	What I want my learner to know
• Compares larger numbers up to 100 (e.g., double, half, *n* less, *n* more). • Understands that a number can be made of several smaller parts. • Compares numbers by identifying double and half. • Uses the number of digits to help compare and relate numbers to one another. • Estimates measurements with reasoning and explains the reasoning. • Uses a variety of thinking tools, including open models, to demonstrate thinking. • Chooses thinking tools based on the situation.	• Compare larger numbers up to 1,000. • Understand that a number can be broken into equal groups. • Relate double and half to multiply by 2 and divide by 2. • Use digits to the right of the decimal to help compare and relate numbers to one another. • Estimate measurements using a variety of strategies and use estimates to monitor reasonableness throughout the problem solving process. • Develop "mental" models as tools "for" thinking.

Learning Experience

A number seems big when you compare it to one benchmark number but seems small when you compare it to a different benchmark number. Use models to show how this is possible.

Student thinking:	Teacher thinking:
Saying: • *I could use a number line.* • *11 is bigger than 10 but a lot smaller than 100.* • *I used dimes to make it easier to see.* *Doing:* • Gathers a collection of coins, base-10 blocks, and relational rods. • Builds physical models using thinking tools.	*Noticing:* • Chooses benchmarks of 10 and 100 and the number 11 to compare. • Draws an open number line with a pencil and uses gestures to break it into sections. • Chooses a small collection of thinking tools (manipulatives). • Represents using models by placing 11 directly beside 10 and 100. *Interpreting:* • Understands that 11 seems big compared to 10 but small compared to 100.

Representing:	
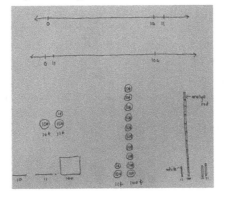	- Uses spatial reasoning to establish where numbers should be placed on an open number line. - Makes critical choices of thinking tools that will best show a comparison of the numbers chosen. - Makes choices while representing to make it easy to justify points. *Confirming:* - *How did you choose your number and benchmarks?* - *How did you decide where each number should go on the number line?* - *Why were the thinking tools you chose a good choice for this situation?* - *How did you plan your representations?* *Responding:* - *How could you describe how much bigger 11 is than 10? How much smaller 11 is than 100?* - *How many times would you have to repeat 11 to get to 100?* - *What equation would describe this relationship?* - *How would your number line change if you changed 100 to 200, 500, or 1,000?*

Additional Learning Experiences to Support Learning Relating

- Make of list of three to five interesting fractions. Put them on a number line. Then, compare some of the fractions.
- Two numbers that are pretty close together when you count a certain way are pretty far apart on a number line. Two different numbers that are pretty far apart when you count a certain way are pretty close on a different number line. Show and tell how each is true.
- Two students are comparing two rectangles. One student says that one shape is a little more than twice as big as the smaller one. The other student says that one shape is about 12 units bigger than the smaller one. What might the rectangles look like?

- Pick a distance that you think you can run. Use a unit to describe the distance that will make it sound like you ran very far. Then, use a unit to describe the distance that will make it sound like you didn't run very far.
- Make an interesting design with pattern blocks. Use a green triangle as a unit to measure your design. Then, repeat measuring your design using a blue rhombus and yellow hexagon as your unit. Compare the results of your measurements.
- A rectangle has twice the length as width. Make this rectangle. Measure the length, width, perimeter, and area of the rectangle. Then, double **one** of the measurements and tell what happens to the other measurements.

Grade 6–10 Learner Experience #1

Learning Intentions: To use number benchmarks to relate fractions.

Success Criteria:

Students will
- think of one number in relation to another using benchmarks
- use prior knowledge to determine meaning from a graphic feature
- draw conclusions based on stated and implied information on the number line

What I know about my learner	What I want my learner to know
<ul><li>Thinks about one number in terms of another.</li><li>Uses, compares, recognizes, and describes whole numbers greater than 1,000.</li><li>Relates numbers proportionally.</li><li>Names and interprets fractions symbolically.</li><li>Creates representations of fractions.</li><li>Names, interprets, and represents decimals with up to two digits to the right of the decimal point.</li><li>Relates and estimates numbers between 1,000 and 100,000 using benchmark numbers.</li></ul>	<ul><li>Relate fractions and decimals using benchmarks.</li><li>Name and interpret numbers between 0 and 1 described as fractions, decimals, or percent.</li><li>Relate equivalent fraction, decimal, and percent descriptions.</li><li>Represent a whole number, fraction, or decimal in two or more forms.</li></ul>

↓

Learning Experience

What might the missing numbers be? How do you know?
What can't they be? How do you know?

Student thinking:	**Teacher thinking:**
Saying: • *I am given 1 on the number line, so I think the other end of the line is 0.* • *The dots have to be between 0 and 0.5.* *Doing:* • Places 0 on the number line. • Places dashes on the number line to represent 0.1, 0.2, 0.3, and 0.4. *Representing:* 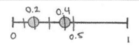 — The numbers might be 0.2 and 0.4 — I know 0.5 is in the middle of 0 and 1 and I know the two numbers have to be less than 0.5 but more than 0 — It can't be 0.1 because it is a little too far from 0 — I think it is 0.4 because the dot is really to 0.5 so it can't be 0.3	*Noticing:* • Places dashes on the number line to validate thinking about what the numbers might be. • Thinks of the dots as decimals in relation to benchmark numbers. *Interpreting:* • Formulates an opinion based on the information provided on the number line. • Demonstrates knowledge of decimals between 0 and 1. • Identifies 0.5 and 1 as benchmark numbers. *Confirming:* • *How did the number line help you relate and order numbers?* • *How did the number 1 help your thinking about what the numbers might be?* *Responding:* • *What might the equivalent fraction be?* • *What might the numbers be if the number line was labeled as 1,000,000?*

Grade 6–10 Learning Experience #2

Learning Intentions: To identify similarities and differences of functions.

Success Criteria:

Students will

- use various features of functions to compare functions
- identify key features of functions
- justify their thinking by reasoning with evidence

What I know about my learner	What I want my learner to know
• Determines other representations of linear and quadratic relations given one representations. • Identifies linear and non-linear functions. • Describes the significance of m and b in $y = mx + b$. • Describes properties of the slopes of lines and line segments. • Describes key features of linear and quadratic functions.	• Apply knowledge and understanding of key features to make comparisons between linear and quadratic functions. • Solve problems involving linear and quadratic equations. • Use appropriate terminology to describe the key features of linear and quadratic equations.

Learning Experience

Which of these equations are most alike? How do you know?

$y = 3x - 6$

$y = 3x^2 + 6x - 24$

$y = 3x + 2$

Student thinking:	Teacher thinking:
Saying: • *The first thing I think of is (1) and (2) because they are both linear.* • *But I think I want to sketch them before I make my final decision.* *Doing:* • *Graphs all three equations by hand.* • *Factors the second equation to determine the zeros.*	*Noticing:* • Graphs equations (1) and (3) by first plotting the y-intercepts and then determining the second point for each by using the value of the slope. • Graphs equation (2) once it is factored. *Interpreting:* • Demonstrates an understanding of the characteristics of linear and quadratic functions.

Representing:

$y = 3x^2 + 6x - 24$

⇓

$y = 3(x^2 + 2x - 8)$

$y = 3(x + 4)(x - 2)$

zeros: $-4, 2$

I think $y = 3x^2 + 6x - 24$ and $y = 3x + 2$ are most alike

- they intersect
- both begin with a 3
- both have an x-intercept of $(2, 0)$
- both have a y-intercept
- both have the same domain

- Makes connections between various representations of a function.

Confirming
- *How did the graphs help you?*
- *How did factoring help you?*
- *How did you determine the minimum value of the quadratic function?*
- *What can you tell me about the domain of all the functions?*

Responding:
- *What other representations might you use?*
- *How are equations (1) and (2) similar? Different?*
- *How are equations (1) and (3) similar? Different?*

Additional Learning Experiences to Support Learning Relating

- How is adding integers the same as adding whole numbers? How is it different?
- How is subtracting integers the same as subtracting whole numbers? How is it different?
- The solution to an equation is $n = -4$. What might the equation be?
- One solution to a quadratic equation is $n = 2$. What might the equation be?

6

Representing

Malik has been teaching for eight years. He recently had a conversation with a parent about their child's progress and finds himself reflecting on the dialogue and the importance of gathering evidence of student thinking and learning from a variety of sources. The parent was very appreciative of the feedback that Malik provided within the first few months of the school year and is eager to further discuss the child's progress. The parent brings various written products to the meeting to guide the conversation about the recent report card grade. Although the parent is content with the grade, an A, the parent is somewhat confused about the child's progress. The parent feels, based on some of the written products the child has brought home, that their child's understanding of various mathematical concepts might not be reflective of the grade.

Malik is eager to share additional evidence with the parent, which is also reflective of the grade most recently issued. As part of the conversation, he shares some of the ways he gathers evidence of student thinking and learning with the parent. Malik includes recent images, videos, and transcribed conversations he had with the child. He also shares examples of success criteria that he uses to assess mathematical thinking. As an example, he shares the following narrative with the parent, which is evidence of the student engaging in reflection as part of their mathematical thinking.

"I recently presented the students with a math task. After spending a few minutes making sense of the problem, your son walked over to the table of manipulatives or thinking tools. I watched him pick up a thinking tool. He held it for a brief moment and then put it down. He then picked up another thinking tool and took it to his desk. He then used that thinking tool to help him represent his thinking and understanding. I was eager to confirm what I had seen, a gesture that represented evidence of reflection, so I asked him why he put down one thinking tool to pick up another. Your son said, 'Sir, I wanted a tool that was going to help me answer the question. It didn't make sense for me to use the tool I first picked up. I wouldn't have been able to represent a part of a fraction accurately. I thought it might work, but then I thought this would work better, and it did'."

The parent now understands that evidence of thinking and learning comes from a variety of different sources, not just written products. Malik recalls the final statement made by the parent, "Thank you for helping me understand that written products are necessary, but not sufficient. I thought only written products mattered and I would have never considered a gesture as possible evidence of thinking. Thank you for helping me better understand my son."

THE IMPORTANT STUFF

- Representations help to make abstract thinking visible.
- Reasoning with representations helps to generalize.
- Representing is a way of communicating thinking and understanding.
- Multiple representations provide opportunities to make connections between the different ways of thinking about things.
- Different representations tell us different things about mathematical thoughts.
- There are different ways to represent mathematical thoughts.
- Different representations can be useful for different purposes.

(NRC, 2001)

Making Sense of Representing

"When students gain access to mathematical representations and the ideas they represent, they have a set of tools that significantly expand their capacity to think." NCTM, 2000, p. 67

Students engage in reasoning and use representations to communicate their mathematical thinking and understanding of mathematical concepts and skills. When students are reasoning they are recognizing relationships, making generalizations, making conjectures, and verifying conclusions (Small, 2017). When they are communicating, students are making their thinking visible and providing opportunities to build upon their own thinking as well as the thinking of others. Representing, simply stated, is about capturing a mathematical thought. Once captured, representations can then be used as a springboard to think more deeply about the mathematical thought. For example, students think more deeply when they reflect on the representations, make connections, and synthesize their understanding. By reflecting on the representations, students think about their own thought process as part of monitoring their own learning. As they reflect they also think about how to expand their knowledge and understanding to make connections so they can transfer learning to new contexts (Fiore & Lebar, 2017). When students synthesize, they are combining and integrating ideas that lead to the creation of a new understanding. By posing thinking stems such as "I used to think . . . now I think . . .," students have an opportunity to synthesize their understanding through their representations.

"Representations should be treated as essential elements in supporting students' understanding of mathematical concepts and relationships; in communicating mathematical approaches, arguments, and understanding to one's self and to others; in recognizing connections among related mathematical concepts; and in applying mathematics to realistic problem situations through modeling." NCTM, 2000, p. 67

Representing mathematical thoughts plays an important role in teaching and learning. Students have the important role of reflecting on their mathematical thoughts and making their understanding visible. How students choose to represent their thoughts helps to clarify their understanding and tells us different things. For example, a student may represent their thinking of the number 30 by using an array (see Figure 6.1). The representation helps us understand that a student is thinking of equal groups in a rectangular fashion. The representation also tells us that a student is able to think of a number as the product of two numbers.

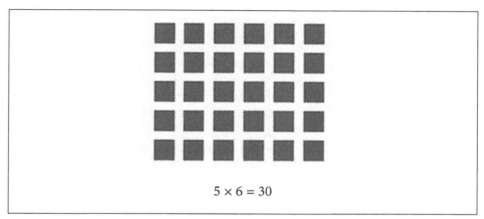

$5 \times 6 = 30$

Figure 6.1: Array Representing 30

Another student may represent their thinking of 30 using a number line (see Figure 6.2). This representation helps us understand that a student has an understanding of the use of benchmark numbers to help order and compare numbers.

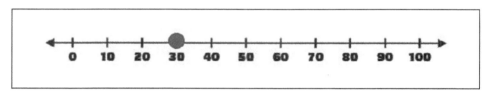

Figure 6.2: Number Line Representing 30

Both representations clarify the student's thinking about the number 30 and provide opportunities for students to make connections between the two representations. By posing further questions, such as, "How could you use a number line to show the mathematical thought represented in the array?" or "How could you use the number line to represent the product of 5 and 6?," students are able to make connections and deepen their understanding of number. We therefore have the important role of creating learning experiences where students have an opportunity to represent their thinking and understanding about a mathematical idea in a number of ways. This includes encouraging students to represent their mathematical thoughts in ways that make sense to them. How a student represents their thoughts helps us determine where they are along a mathematical learning progression and plan next steps based on this understanding.

Consider again the representations shown in Figures 6.1 and 6.2. If the learning intention focused on thinking of numbers as factors of other numbers to enhance students' understanding of number, the first representation demonstrates an understanding of the learning intention. However, the second representation would require further prompting through the use of questioning to elicit further thinking to help us to determine where a student is along the learning continuum, such as "How else might you represent the number 30?" or "How might you represent 30 using multiplication?" (see Figure 6.3).

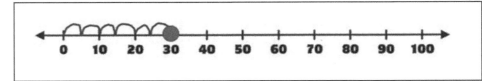

Figure 6.3: *Representing 30 on a Number Line Using Multiplication*

Ways of Representing

Representations help students organize their mathematical thoughts about concepts and help us to gain insights into their ways of interpreting and thinking about mathematics concepts and skills. Earlier we considered how learning progressions help us to better understand our mathematical learners so we can plan for meaningful learning experiences that focus on specific mathematical concepts. For instance, in Chapter 4 we explored how the concept of counting develops along a learning progression. Similar to the concept of counting, the skill of representing follows a learning progression.

Students' mathematical representations tend to progress from concrete to abstract. In the early years, students will often represent their thinking about numbers and operations with numbers using concrete objects, such as counters or 10-frames. In the middle grades, students' representations reflect their understanding of more abstract concepts such as rates or linear relationships. Finally, in secondary school, students use conventional representations, such as algebraic representations, as a means of expressing their understanding of even more abstract concepts.

Using Thinking Tools to Represent

Thinking tools, commonly referred to as manipulatives, help students to construct knowledge. Thinking tools are often described as concrete materials that are used to represent student thinking. Students construct meaning as they explore, investigate, create, and discover while using thinking tools. Thinking tools include manufactured items such as base-10 blocks, relational rods, fraction strips, algebra tiles, counters, or 10-frames, but also include items such as buttons, beans, sand, and water. For example, base-10 blocks are typically used to show how the place value system relates to the base 10 system (Small, 2017) (see Figure 6.4).

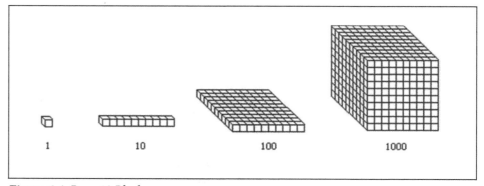

Figure 6.4: *Base-10 Blocks*

Throughout this book we have embedded many learning experiences that promote sense making. The thinking tools were purposefully selected to represent our understanding of the key number concepts of counting, quantity, and relating. It is important to note that simply providing the materials in the learning space does not ensure that students will engage in learning about mathematics concepts. Thinking tools provide opportunities for thinking and learning when they are purposefully used to make links between the concrete material and the mathematical idea they represent. Thinking tools support student thinking and learning by providing:

- models students can refer to even when the thinking tools are no longer present;
- a reason for students to work collaboratively as they engage in mathematical learning experiences;
- a reason for students to engage in conversations about mathematical concepts; and
- a level of autonomy, since students can work with the tools without teacher guidance.

(Small, 2017)

Opportunity for Reflection

Linking cubes can be used when making number comparisons. What mathematical idea would be supported using a 10-frame?

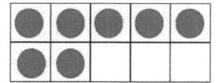

Using Gestures to Represent

As teachers, we look for and check for evidence of understanding through a variety of modalities. We often rely on seeing and hearing, but movement can also be used to communicate thinking and understanding (Moss & Bruce, 2016). When we reflect on the vignette in the chapter opener, Malik relied on the movement made by the student, which he interpreted as *the student engaging in reflecting and reasoning*. To confirm his thinking, he asked the student questions. Once confirmed, he could consider the movement he noticed as evidence of the student's thinking.

As another example, consider a student who is using a number line to communicate understanding of the difference between 18 and 6. The student places his finger on 6 and then moves his finger along the number line repeatedly by 2, until he stops at 18 and responds "12." In this example, the intention of the movement is to represent the strategy of skip counting. Each of the six skips represents counting on by 2. Recognizing the movement made by the student's hand, the teacher is able to better understand the student's thinking.

Gestures or movements can represent mathematical ideas such as adding or subtracting, but they can also be used to express spatial ideas (e.g., rotations) when language is not yet accessible. It is important to distinguish between gestures that represent thinking and mathematical understanding (e.g., representational gestures, such as bringing the hands together to represent addition) and those that may not (e.g., emblematic gestures such as waving "hello") (McNeill, 2008; Alibali, 2005).

"Whether we are aware of it or not, we regularly use gestures to express ourselves as well as to better understand the intentions of other."
Moss & Bruce, 2016, p. 47

Using Strategies and Models to Represent

Although there are differences between strategies and models, we feel it is necessary to discuss them together. Similar to the notion of it being difficult to separate instruction and assessment when we discuss teaching and learning, it is also difficult to separate strategies and models when engaging in conversations about representing. Strategies enhance mathematical models when students represent their mathematical thoughts. Consider the representation shown in Figure 6.5 that the student uses to communicate their mathematical thinking when asked to reflect on the sum of 54 + 38. The student uses base-10 materials to model their thoughts, which incorporate the strategy of splitting. The student splits 54 into 5 tens and 4 ones, splits 38 into 3 tens and 8 ones, adds 2 ones and 8 ones, and then adds the partial sums: 50 + 30 + 10 + 2.

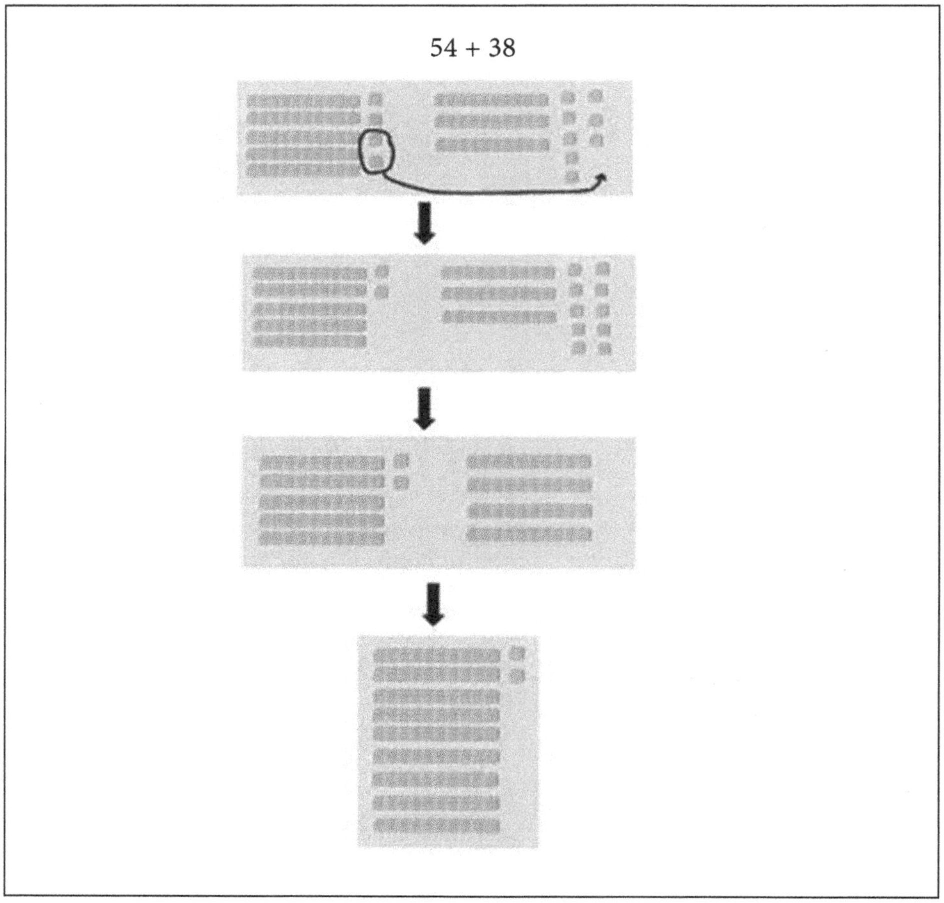

Figure 6.5: *Using Base-10 Materials to Model Addition*

Encouraging students to use visual images or drawings to represent their thinking enhances student learning. Consider, for example, the use of a concept circle where the learner records pictures, numbers, symbols, or words that represent that concept. Concept circles provide opportunities for students to make connections between mathematical concepts and reinforce that there are different ways to represent mathematical ideas. Figure 6.6 shows a concept circle representing a student's understanding of the concept of $\frac{3}{4}$.

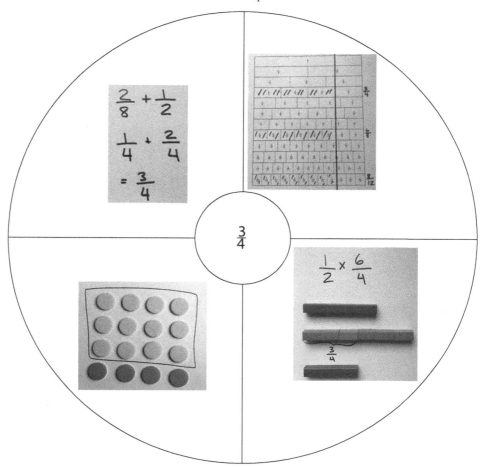

Figure 6.6: Concept Circle Representing the Concept of $\frac{3}{4}$

Using Prompting to Think about Representing

"Providing useful images and encouraging schematics drawings is of tremendous importance in supporting student learning." *Van de Walle et al., 2017, p. 103*

It is important to consider how we can encourage students to represent their thinking and the thinking of others. Prompting through the use of thinking stems and prompting questions provides students with opportunities to further reflect on their thoughts and communicate their thinking (Fiore & Lebar, 2017). Consider how the thinking stems and prompting questions identified below can be applied to a wide range of opportunities across different math strands.

Thinking stems:

I can show my thinking by . . .
I chose . . . to show my thinking about . . . because . . .
The relationship between this representation and that representation is . . .
I think this representation is more effective because . . .
This representation made me think of . . .
This representation makes my thinking about . . . clearer . . .

Prompting questions:

How might you show your thinking in a different way?
What are the connections between the different representations? What made you choose that representation?
Why do you think this representation best represents that mathematical idea?
What are the pros and cons of this thinking tool?
How did that gesture help you understand . . .?

How Will We Know Our Students Understand Representing?

We will know that students are intentionally making their thinking visible through the use of various representations when we hear or see them doing the following:

☐ Using thinking tools, gestures, or models to communicate mathematical thoughts.
☐ Creating visual representations of their mathematical thoughts.
☐ Using symbols to model a mathematical idea or generalization.
☐ Representing their thinking in a variety of ways.
☐ Making connections between various representations.
☐ Making connections between representations and mathematical ideas.
☐ Recognizing how representations can be useful for different purposes.

The progression shown in Figure 6.7 demonstrates a simplified version of how students develop a sense of representing over time as they move from foundational understanding to more sophisticated understanding. It is possible and likely that students will be working in more than one phase at a time. Although synthesized from research, this progression is an approximation of how students might develop over time and is not intended to be a fulsome picture.

- Recognizes different ways of representing whole numbers to 10.
- Recognizes equivalence between different concrete and/or pictorial display of number to 10.
- Models simple repeating patterns in a variety of ways.
- Represents common 2-D shapes and single faces from a 3-D figure.
- Represents measurements in simple ways.
- Creates simple concrete and picture graphs based on categories developed by someone else.

- Creates concrete representations of different decompositions of the same number.
- Changes ordinal position by changing viewpoint or representation.
- Creates concrete models of familiar ratios.
- Creates concrete and pictorial representations of familiar equivalent fractions.
- Translates simple repeating patterns from one medium to another.
- Represents 2-D shapes and approximations of 3-D figures.
- Recognizes that 3-D figures look different depending on the view.
- Represents measurements using appropriate non-standard units.
- Creates simple bar graphs and pictographs.

- Represents numbers using arrays and describes a number in terms of a unit other than one.
- Represents simple ratios using concrete and pictorial models.
- Creates concrete and pictorial representations of less familiar equivalent fractions.
- Represents numbers using different models to highlight different things about a number.
- Translates a broader range of repeating patterns (e.g., a two-attribute pattern) from one medium to another.
- Represents 3-D figures using nets and skeletons from multiple perspectives.
- Represent measurements using common standard units.
- Creates pictographs, bar graphs, and broken line graphs with given scales.

- Represents numbers as multiples and factors of one another.
- Represents whole numbers as decimal multiples of numbers (e.g., 2,100,000 as 2.1 million).
- Solves ratio, fraction, and decimal problems symbolically.
- Represents fractions, decimals, and percent interchangeably based on the context.
- Represents complex pattern rules with words.
- Represents 3-D figures using isometric drawings from multiple perspectives.
- Creates nets for a given 3-D figure.
- Represents and converts measurements based on the context.
- Creates pictographs, bar graphs, and broken line graphs and chooses scales.
- Creates circle graphs and stem-and-leaf plots.

Figure 6.6: Sample Progression for Representing

Adapted from Small, 2005; Clements & Sarama, 2014

Learning Experiences

The following learning experiences are organized into grade bands: Kindergarten–Grade 2, Grade 3–5, and Grade 6–10. They are designed to demonstrate how you can use your students as resources to plan for and deliver responsive tasks based on a sample progression of learning. We have used learning experiences from across the strands of mathematics to help key number ideas emerge.

Kindergarten–Grade 2 Learning Experience #1

Learning Intentions: To represent numbers in different ways.

Success Criteria:

Students will

- represent the same number in different ways
- compare a number to a benchmark number
- explain what some representations highlight about a number

What I know about my learner	What I want my learner to know
• Recognizes different ways of representing whole numbers to 10, including subitizing common patterns. • Represents single-digit numbers with drawings and using manipulatives. • Lines up two sets of objects to identify which is more or less or if they are the same. • Creates and extends AB and AAB patterns using familiar materials. • Draws reasonable approximations of triangles, squares, rectangles, and circles. • Orders drawings from shortest to longest. • Represents the results from a simple survey on a tracking sheet provided by an educator. • Represents survey results on a concrete graph or pictograph as directed by an educator.	• Use familiar models to show a number. • Tell some information about what a representation of a number highlights about the number. • Represent a measurement with an approximation of the result. • Represent more complex patterns with increasing sophistication of attributes. • Compare two representations of the same shape to find similarities and differences. • Represent the results from a survey independently. • Choose a representation for a survey or experiment that makes sense for the situation.

Learning Experience
Choose a number that is important to you. Show it in lots of different ways.

Student thinking:	Teacher thinking:
Saying: • I am 6 years old. • I'm gathering lots of materials: 1, 2, 3, 4, 5, 6. *Doing:* • Touches manipulatives while saying a counting sequence. • Grabs a collection of five thinking tools. • Reviews the physical representation several times while creating the pictorial representation. *Representing:*  (Some teacher scribing) 	*Noticing:* • Draws some, counts some, adds more, counts again. • Used 5-frame, 10-frame, shapes, pictorial, written, numeral, and other representations. • Builds different structures for 6 with the same materials. • Represents 6 as a time of day. *Interpreting:* • Has one-to-one tagging and synchrony but does not always track where ended during previous counting. • Understands that a number can be represented many different ways. • Understands that 6 can be shown in one row or two rows. • Recognizes real-life contexts for the use of the number 6. *Confirming:* • *How do you know for sure there are 6 in each representation?* • *(Pointing to the two cube representations) How are these two the same and different?* • *When do you use the number 6 in your everyday life?* *Responding:* • *Which two ways are most alike? Different?* • *Which way shows that 6 is a little bit bigger than 5? Smaller than 10?* • *(Pointing to the 2 × 3 cube representation) When might it be helpful to think about 6 this way?*

Kindergarten–Grade 2 Learning Experience #2

Learning Intentions: To represent a triangle in lots of different ways.

Success Criteria:

Students will

- represent triangles using their properties
- explain features that a triangle must have (properties) and a triangle can have (attributes)
- explain why another shape is not a triangle and how it would have to change to become a triangle

What I know about my learner	What I want my learner to know
• Uses one-to-one tagging and synchrony to count collections of objects and sides on shapes. • Organizes a collection of objects in a row to make it easy to count. • Tracks a starting point when counting sides on a 2-D shape. • Quickly recognizes different representations of familiar shapes including triangle, square, rectangle, and circle. • Represents 2-D shapes with approximations. • Talks about a shape by mentioning a few attributes. • Represents the results from a survey using an educator model or organizer. • Uses familiar models to represent a number.	• Conserve number in order to count on. • Track counted objects. • Recognize attributes of less familiar shapes. • Draw or create very different looking shapes that have the same name (e.g., triangle, hexagon). • Use more precise tools and/or materials to create representations of shapes. • Compare two representations of the same shape to find similarities and differences. • Represent the results from a survey independently. • Choose a representation for a survey or experiment that makes sense for the situation.

Learning Experience

(Provide Geoboards and elastics.) Make lots of triangles that look different from each other. Then, on a second geoboard, make some shapes that are almost triangles but not quite.

Student thinking:	Teacher thinking:
Saying: • *1, 2, 3.* • *That's an upside-down triangle.* • *This one is two triangles stuck together, see?*	*Noticing:* • Makes each triangle with three sides. • Makes one small and some big triangles.

Doing:
- Moves each elastic several times before adding another elastic.
- Adds the elastic to a different place on the geoboard each time.
- Touches each vertex and mouths a word.

Representing:

Triangles:

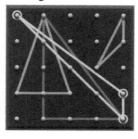

Not quite triangles:

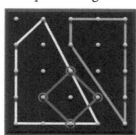

- Thinks that a triangle is upside down.
- Uses different colors to make the shapes.
- Makes each of the "not quite" triangles with four sides.

Interpreting:
- Understands that a triangle must have three sides.
- Might think that it is not a triangle if the point is facing down.
- Knows that size and color do not matter when making triangles.
- Knows that 4 is close to 3, so a shape with four sides is close to a triangle.

Confirming:
- *How did you make sure that each shape was a triangle?*
- *Which two are most alike?*
- *Which one is not a lot like the others? Why?*
- *What makes these "not quite" triangles?*

Responding:
- *If someone said they were looking at a triangle but you couldn't see it, what would you know for sure about it? What would you be not so sure about?*
- *How might you change these shapes to make them into triangles?*

Additional Learning Experiences to Support Learning Representing

- How are the numbers 5 and 10 similar? How are they different?
- What happens when you add 1 to a counting number? Show your thinking in two different ways.
- A bunch of different cookies are on a plate. How could you sort the cookies into groups?

Grade 3–5 Learning Experience #1

Learning Intentions: To show that different representations of data can highlight different things about a graph.

Success Criteria:

Students will
- choose a graph that makes sense for the data being collected
- analyze and interpret what the graph highlights about the data being displayed
- explain the similarities and differences between two graphs displaying the same data

What I know about my learner	What I want my learner to know
• Represents numbers, shapes, and patterns in many ways and explains the similarities and differences between the representations. • Creates concrete and pictorial representations of familiar equivalent fractions. • Translates simple repeating and growing patterns from one medium to another. • Represents 2-D shapes and approximations of 3-D figures. • Recognizes that 3-D figures look different depending on the view. • Creates a variety of graphs including concrete graphs, pictographs, bar and double-bar graphs, and stem-and-leaf graphs. • Uses the conventions of graph-making including using a scale that fits the data. • Analyzes data by recognizing the most and the least. • Determines the mode and median of a small set of data.	• Represent operations using open models that make thinking clear. • Find equivalence among more complicated fractions and represent them with standard notation. • Represent the same pattern in multiple ways and analyze and compare the representations. • Use visualization to manipulate shapes in space and predict the outcomes of transformations. • Critically assess, choose, and create the best type of graph for the purpose and audience. • Analyze data to identify the shape and trends. • Compare and contrast the use of different graphs by explaining what each type of graph highlights about the data being presented. • Explain the impact on mode and median of adding certain data values.

Learning Experience
Conduct a survey or experiment with two different groups of students. Collect the data. Display the data in two different ways.

Student thinking:	Teacher thinking:
Saying: • *I am doing an experiment: "What is your favorite outdoor activity?"* • *I am asking a Grade 3 class and a Grade 4 class.* • *The Grade 4s like basketball more than the Grade 3s.* *Doing:* • Gathers a clipboard, pencil, and paper. • Draws a chart on paper. • Talks to many students within classroom and another classroom down the hall. *Representing:* 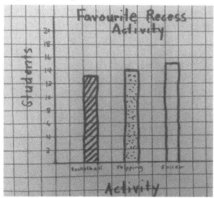 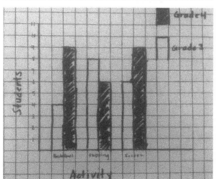	*Noticing:* • Chooses a single- and double-bar graph. • Uses a scale of 0 to 11 and 0 to 22 on the graphs. • Chooses a Grade 3 and 4 class. • Uses grid paper for the graph. • Includes a title, labels, and a scale. • Includes a legend for the double-bar graph. • Uses different designs on the bars. *Interpreting:* • Matches a graph to the situation. • Assesses the results and the grid paper and chooses an appropriate scale. • Chooses an accessible audience. • Uses the conventions of graph making. • Creates contrast on a graph to help interpret the data. *Confirming:* • *What did you do?* • *What criteria did you use to help you choose the types of graphs?* • *What were you sure to include on your graph?* • *How does that information help your audience?* *Responding:* • *What does the bar graph show really well about your data that the double-bar graph doesn't show as well?* • *What does the double-bar graph show really well about your data that the bar graph doesn't show as well?* • *When is each graph helpful?* • *Why might someone choose to display data one way over another?*

Grade 3–5 Learning Experience #2

Learning Intentions: To represent fractions in different ways.

Success Criteria:

Students will

- justify how a representation matches the fraction
- tell some of the things that the representation highlights about the fraction
- explain why the whole matters when comparing fractions

What I know about my learner	What I want my learner to know
• Skip counts forwards and backwards by different numbers to establish a quantity. • Relates numbers into the hundreds to real-life contexts. • Equates decimals in common real-life contexts. • Identifies common unit fractions. • Represents unit fractions on different models. • Names the value of each digit in a two- and three-digit number.	• Count forwards and backwards by decimals and fractions to determine quantities. • Relate numbers into the thousands to real-life contexts. • Equate decimal tenths to an area of one-tenth the size of the whole or a distance of one-tenth the total distance. • Identify fractions as a number of unit fractions (e.g., $\frac{3}{4}$ is three one-fourths). • Represent proper fractions on different models and explain how each model highlights different things about the fraction. • Rename whole numbers to 1,000 (e.g., 1,000 is 10 hundreds or 100 tens).

↓

Learning Experience

Choose one of these fractions: $\frac{1}{3}$ $\frac{3}{4}$ $\frac{2}{3}$ $\frac{1}{4}$

Create lots of representations for the fraction you chose.

Student thinking:	Teacher thinking:
Saying: • *Half is about here, and halfway between $\frac{1}{2}$ and 1 is about here.* • *Three quarters sounds like money.* • *A quarter to one is like three quarters after twelve on a clock.*	*Noticing:* • Uses several different models to show the fraction. • Uses models to show a fraction of a region and a fraction of a set.

Doing:
- Looks around the room.
- Scans other students' papers.
- Gathers thinking tools including fraction circles, money, pattern blocks, and fraction strips.

Representing:

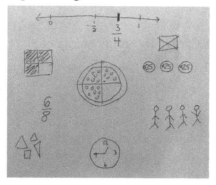

- Models the fraction on a number line.
- Models $\frac{3}{4}$ as $\frac{6}{8}$.

Interpreting:
- Understands that $\frac{3}{4}$ can mean many different things depending on the whole.
- Understands when to use a fraction.
- Understands that $\frac{3}{4}$ can describe a distance.
- Has an abstract understanding of equivalent fractions.

Confirming:
- *How are your representations the same? How are they different?*
- *When can you use a fraction?*
- *What two representations do you think are most alike? Why?*
- *How could you show that $\frac{3}{4}$ is the same as $\frac{6}{8}$?*

Responding:
- *Which representations show that $\frac{3}{4}$ is the same as three one-fourths?*
- *Which representations also show $\frac{1}{4}$? Why do you think that makes sense?*

Additional Learning Experiences to Support Learning Representing

- Draw a picture that shows the connection between addition and multiplication.
- Pick a fraction and represent it in three different ways.
- Is $n - 2 = 16$ the same as $2 - n = 16$? Show how you know.
- A shape has an area of 30 square units. What might the shape look like?

Grade 6–10 Learner Experience #1

Learning Intentions: To use exponent rules to simplify algebraic expressions.

Success Criteria:

Students will

- recognize when to use exponent laws
- represent a whole number using an exponent
- use the exponent laws to simplify algebraic expressions
- justify their thinking by reasoning with evidence

What I know about my learner	What I want my learner to know
<ul><li>Represents perfect square numbers.</li><li>Explains the relationship between exponential notation and the measurement of area and volume.</li><li>Expresses repeated multiplication using exponential notation.</li><li>Represents whole numbers using powers of 10.</li><li>Evaluates algebraic expression involving exponents.</li><li>States the exponent rules for multiplying and dividing monomials.</li></ul>	<ul><li>Apply the exponent rules in expressions involving one and two variables.</li><li>Express whole numbers in exponential form.</li><li>Apply the exponent rules in expressions involving whole numbers.</li><li>Extend the multiplication rule to derive and understand the power rule.</li></ul>

Learning Experience

Why might it be helpful to represent $\frac{24 \times 256}{32}$ in a different way to perform the calculation?

Student thinking:	Teacher thinking:
Saying: - *We learned about exponents and exponent laws to help us find answers a few days ago.* - *I am pretty sure 32 and 256 can be expressed as exponents with base 2 . . . for sure 32 can.* *Doing:* - Uses a calculator to guess and check an exponent equivalent to 256 and 32.	*Noticing:* - Represents 32 and 256 using exponents. - Does not use the exponent laws to simplify. *Interpreting:* - Recognizes that exponents are different representations of whole numbers. - Understands why the exponent laws can be used to simplify numerical expressions.

Representing:

*we learned about exponent laws to make things more easy to calculate

*so if the question was $\dfrac{16 \times 256}{32}$

I would have to multiply and divide big numbers

*But I think changing the numbers to exponents would be better

*because one of the exponents is 2^4 I think the other should have $2s$ in it

*like 256 is 2^8 and 32 is 2^5

*so the different way is $\dfrac{2^4 \times 2^8}{2^5}$

Confirming:
- *What helped you decide which representation to use?*
- *Why did you express 32 and 256 as an exponent with a base of 2?*
- *What are exponents?*
- *How have you used exponents in the past?*

Responding:
- *If 2^4 was expressed as 16, how would that have changed your thinking?*
- *How else could you represent the expression?*
- *Create a similar question and share it with a partner.*

Grade 6–10 Learning Experience #2

Learning Intentions: To represent quadratic function in different ways.

Success Criteria:

Students will
- identify the key features of a graph of a parabola
- describe the key features of a parabola
- determine algebraic representations of quadratic equations
- justify their thinking by reasoning with evidence

What I know about my learner	What I want my learner to know
<ul><li>Expands and simplifies second degree polynomials expressions.</li><li>Factors simple trinomials of the form $x^2 + bx + c$.</li><li>Recognizes that quadratic equations can be graphically represented as a parabola.</li><li>Determines second differences to determine if a table of values represents a quadratic relationship.</li><li>Identifies the key features of a graph of a parabola.</li></ul>	<ul><li>Use appropriate terminology to describe key features of a graph of a parabola.</li><li>Compare graphical representations of a quadratic relation in the form $x^2 + bx + c$ and the same relation in factored form $y = (x - r)(x - s)$</li><li>Describe connections between an algebraic representation and the graph of a quadratic relation.</li><li>Express $y = ax^2 + bx + c$ in the form $y = a(x - h)^2 + k$ by completing the square.</li></ul>

Learning Experience

What might the equation be?

What makes you say that?

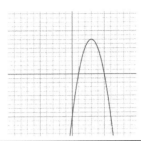

Student thinking:	Teacher thinking:
Saying: • *I know it is a quadratic equation because the shape of its graph is a parabola.* • *I know the graph opens down so it begins with a negative.* *Doing:* • Identifies a scale for the x-axis and the y-axis. • Identifies the vertex and the zeros of the graph. *Representing:*	*Noticing:* • Selects various forms of quadratic equations. • Uses stated and implied information to draw conclusions about key features of quadratics. *Interpreting:* • Applies knowledge and understanding of the key features of a graph of a parabola to develop a strategy to determine an algebraic expression.

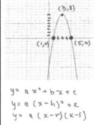

• if I make the x and y axis go up by 1 then my zeros are (1,0) and (5,0)

• I also know that the vertex is (3,8)

$y = a x^2 + b x + c$

$y = a (x - h)^2 + k$

$y = a (x - r)(x - s)$

$y = a (x - 1)(x - 5)$

$8 = a (3 - 1)(3 - 5)$

$8 = a (2)(-2)$

$8 = -4a$

$-2 = a$

• I can use the vertex as another point to help me find a

$y = -2 (x - 1)(x - 5)$

• using the factored form I could use the zeros and I know the parabola opens down and there is a -2

Confirming:
• *What information does the graph provide?*
• *How did you decide which algebraic representation you would use?*

Responding:
• *When would it make sense to use the other algebraic representations?*
• *In what ways are the algebraic equations related?*
• *What strategy might you have used if the zeros were not clearly identifiable?*

Additional Learning Experiences to Support Learning Representing

• Two polynomials add up to $12x^2 - 4x + 10$. What might they be?
• How might the relationship $(a + b)(a - b) = a^2 - b^2$ help you find the product of 42 and 38?

Consolidating Our Professional Learning

Providing students with meaningful learning experiences means giving them opportunities to reflect on previous learning and personal experiences, develop understanding, and consolidate learning. This chapter synthesizes the important ideas addressed throughout this book as part of consolidating our professional learning.

Summary of Our Thinking Related to the Teaching and Learning of Mathematics

The learning experiences presented in this book reflect research-informed practices. Recent research, specifically focusing on the teaching and learning of mathematics, has provided educators with opportunities to reflect on their beliefs and practices about what constitutes mathematics and how we should engage our students with mathematics. Over the past three to four decades, educators have deepened their knowledge and understanding of the many facets associated with the teaching and learning of mathematics. Such topics include, but are not limited to:

- the role of "rich" mathematics tasks to support differentiation;
- supporting mathematical thinking;
- professional noticing of students' mathematical thinking;
- using "effective questions";
- using assessment *for*, *as*, and *of* learning to inform instruction;
- using math talk;
- engaging students using thinking tools;
- teaching through problem-solving; and
- the role of learning progressions.

The learning experiences embedded within this book were purposefully designed to develop and deepen student understanding of mathematics concepts and skills so they develop a sense of number and have *number sense*. When students share the perspective of learning mathematics for number sense, they rely on mathematical thinking to build understanding. When teachers share the perspective of teaching mathematics for number sense, they embrace meaningful learning environments.

When we reflect on teaching and learning, specifically student learning, knowledge and understanding are necessary but not sufficient. The intention is for students to apply and transfer their sense of number to better understand how mathematics is used in the world around them. Mathematics then becomes a way of thinking about things. When students view mathematics as a way of thinking about things, they might be more inclined to ask and think about questions such as:

- How is mathematics used in social and political contexts?
- How might mathematics help me make sense of a situation?
- What are the connections between math and other subject areas?
- How can I help others see the power of mathematics outside of the classroom?

Parallel to student learning is teacher learning. Professional learning experiences designed to deepen our knowledge and understanding of how effective practices promote meaningful learning experiences are integral to teaching and learning. Although knowledge and understanding of effective practices are necessary, they are not sufficient. It is when we apply and transfer our knowledge as part of our daily practices that we foster mathematical learning experiences that enhance students' mathematical thinking and develop students' sense of number. As part of the transfer of knowledge, we are more inclined to ask questions that reflect our professional wonderings such as:

- What do I need to know about my students personally? Professionally?
- How do the learning experiences I have planned support student thinking and understanding?
- Why is this learning happening at this time?
- How will I know students have learned it?
- How do the learning experiences align with the big ideas? The bigger ideas?
- How will I gather evidence of student thinking and learning?
- How might I structure a learning goal to incorporate thinking skills and mathematical concepts and skills?
- What are possible student solutions?
- How might I respond when a student does ... or says ...?
- How might I enhance students' sense of number across the strands?
- How might the "important stuff" support the development of mathematical concepts and skills?

These questions help us to both know our learners and know ourselves as learners of mathematics so that collectively, with our students, we can *make sense of number*. Making sense of number provides students with the opportunity to make sense of mathematics and view mathematics as a way of thinking about things.

Seven Key Concepts

By emphasizing seven key concepts as part of the consolidation process, we can transfer and apply our knowledge and understanding of effective practices to support the teaching and learning of mathematics as part of our daily practice. Each key concept is addressed as a purpose statement to incorporate teacher actions and intended student outcomes. Note that each purpose statement was developed by first considering students' learning needs—gathering and analyzing evidence from a variety of sources—before selecting actions to address those needs. The goal is to provide examples of purpose statements or theories of action that we can use as part of our personal professional learning journey.

Key concept #1: If we engage in professional learning—whether informal or formal—that shifts our thinking and practice to address an identified student learning need, then students will be able to learn something new in a different way.

Key concept #2: If we engage in professional noticing to gather evidence of student thinking and learning, then students will be inclined to make their thinking visible.

Key concept #3: If we develop an understanding of and use learning progressions to purposely plan for meaningful learning experiences, then all students will be able to engage with mathematics.

Key concept #4: If we engage in reflective practice to make connections between our thinking and our students' thinking, then students will see themselves as part of the curriculum.

Key concept #5: If we develop and use learning intentions to align meaningful learning experiences to the "important stuff," then students will view mathematics as more than just rules and procedures.

Key concept #6: If we plan for and implement learning experiences that provide students with opportunities to engage in mathematical thinking, then students will develop an understanding of mathematical concepts.

Key concept #7: If we plan for learning experiences that are purposefully designed to elicit mathematical thinking, then students will better understand the role of mathematics in the world around them.

Appendix A: Student Profile Template

STUDENT PROFILE

Name: _____   Age: _____

Grade: _____

School: _____

Number of Credits Accumulated: _____   Date: _____

Sources of Information
(Identify sources of information and assessments to be conducted.
Check box and note date when a source has been reviewed or a new assessment completed.)

Review of OSR, including previous report cards _____	Interest and/or learning style inventory _____
Consultation with parents _____	Work samples, assignments, projects _____
Consultation with previous and current teachers _____	Portfolios _____
Consultation with support team _____	Teacher-student conferences _____
Classroom observation checklist _____	Peer and self assessments _____
Educational assessments (e.g., pretests related to particular curriculum expectations) _____	Other (specify) _____

Findings from Information Sources and Assessments – Strengths and Areas of Need

Current achievement levels, learning skills/work habits and readiness to learn	Learning styles/preferences and needs, interests, social/emotional strengths and needs	Other relevant information

Assessment and Instruction

Considerations for Instructional Strategies	Considerations for Assessments	Available Resources and Supports

Source: Ontario Ministry of Education, 2013; http://www.edu.gov.on.ca/eng/general/elemsec/speced/LearningforAll2013.pdf

Pembroke Publishers © 2018 *Making Sense of Number, K-10* by Mary Fiore and Ryan Tackaberry ISBN 978-1-55138-332-3

References

Alibali, M. W. (2005) "Gesture in Spatial Cognition: Expressing, Communicating, and Thinking about Spatial Information" *Spatial Cognition & Computation, 5*(4), 307–331.

Anthony, A., & Walshaw, M. (2009) "Characteristics of Effective Teaching of Mathematics: A View from the West" *Journal of Mathematics Education, 2*(2), 147–164.

Ball, D. (2011) "Foreword" In M. G. Sherin, V. R. Jacobs, & R. A. Philip (Eds.), *Mathematics Teacher Noticing: Seeing Through Teachers' Eyes.* New York, NY: Taylor and Francis.

Ball, D., Hill, C., & Bass, H. (2005) "Knowing Mathematics For Teaching: Who Knows Mathematics Well Enough to Teach Third Grade and How Can we Decide?" *American Educator, 29*(1), 14–17, 20–22, 43–46.

Beck, C., & Kosnik, C. (2014) *Growing as a Teacher.* The Netherlands: Sense Publishers.

Beswick, K. (2005) "The Beliefs/Practice Connection in Broadly Defined Contexts" *Mathematics Education Research Journal, 17*(2), 39–68.

Boaler, J. (2015) "Fluency with Fear: Research Evidence on the Best Ways to Learn Math Facts" Youcubed at Stanford University. Retrieved from https://www.youcubed.org/evidence/fluency-without-fear/

Brookhart, S. (2010) *How to Assess Higher-Order Thinking Skills in Your Classroom.* Alexandria, VA: ASCD.

Bryant, J. (1999) "Thinking Mathematically" *The International Journal of Creativity & Problem Solving, 9*(1), 47–57.

Burton, L. (1984) "Mathematical Thinking: The Struggle for Meaning" *Journal for Research in Mathematics Education, 15*(1), 35–49.

Chance, P. (1986) *Thinking in the Classroom: A Survey of Programs.* New York, NY: Teachers College, Columbia University.

Clements, D. H., & Sarama, J. (2014) *Learning and Teaching Early Math: The Learning Trajectories Approach.* 2nd ed. New York, NY: Routledge.

Darling-Hammond, L., Chung Wei, R., Andree, A., Richardson, N., & Orphanos, S. (2009) *Professional Learning in the Learning Profession: A Status*

Report on Teacher Development in the United States and Abroad. CA: National Staff Development Council.

Dewey, J. (1933) *How We Think.* New York, NY: Prometheus Press. (Original work published in 1910).

Dowker, A. (2013) "Young Children's Use of Derived Fact Strategies for Addition and Subtraction" *Frontiers in Human Neuroscience, 7,* 924.

Fiore, M., & Lebar, M. (2016) *Four Roles of the Numerate Learner.* Markham, ON: Pembroke Publishers.

Fiore, M., & Lebar, M. (2017) *Moving Math.* Markham, ON: Pembroke Publishers.

Fuson, K. C., Clements, D. H., & Beckman, S. (2009) *Focus in Grade 1: Teaching with Curriculum Focal Points.* Reston, VA: NCTM.

Gelman, R., & Gallistel, C. (1978) *The Child's Understanding of Number.* Cambridge, MA: Harvard University Press.

Hammerness, K., Darling-Hammond, L., Bransford, J., Berliner, D., Cochran-Smith, M., McDonald, M., & Zeichner, K. (2008) "How Teachers Learn and Develop" In L. Darling-Hammond & J. Bansford (Eds.) *Preparing Teachers for a Changing World: What Teachers Should Learn and Be Able To Do* (pp. 358–389). San Francisco, CA: Jossey-Bass.

Hattie, J., Fisher, D., & Frey, N. (2017) *Visible Learning for Mathematics: What Works Best to Optimize Student Learning.* California: Corwin, A Sage Company.

Howden, H. (1989) "Teaching Number Sense" *The Arithmetic Teacher, 36*(6), 6–11. Retrieved from http://www.jstor.org.myaccess.library.utoronto.ca/stable/41194455

Imm, K. L., Fosnot, C., Dolk, M., Jacob, B., & Stylianou, D. (2012) *Learning to Support Young Mathematicians at Work.* Portsmouth, NH: Heinemann.

Jablonka, E. (2014) "Critical Thinking in Mathematics Education" In S. Lerman, B. Sriraman, E. Jablonka, Y. Shimizu, M. Artigue, R. Even, R. Jorgensen,… M. Graven (Eds.). *Encyclopedia of Mathematics Education* (pp. 121–125). Dordrecht: Springer.

Jacob, S. M. (2012) "Mathematical Achievement and Critical Thinking Skills in Asynchronous Discussion Forums" *Procedia - Social and Behavioral Sciences, 31,* 800–804.

Jacobs, V. R., Lamb, L. C., & Philipp, R. A. (2010) "Professional Noticing of Children's Mathematical Thinking" *Journal for Research in Mathematics Education, 41,* 169–202.

Jaworski, B. (2015) "Teaching for Mathematical Thinking: Inquiry in Mathematics Learning and Teaching" *Mathematics Teaching, 248,* 28–34.

Katz, S., & Dack, L. (2013) *Intentional Interruption: Breaking Down the Barriers to Transform Professional Practice.* California: Corwin, A Sage Company.

Krulik, S., & Rudnick, J. A. (1995). *The New Sourcebook for Teaching Reasoning and Problem Solving in Elementary School.* Needham Heights: Allyn dan Bacon.

Lewison, M., Leland, C., & Harste, J. C. (2008) *Creating Critical Classrooms: K–8 Reading and Writing with an Edge.* New York, NY: L. Erlbaum Associates.

Markovits, Z., & Sowder, J. (1994) "Developing Number Sense: An Intervention Study in Grade 7" *Journal for Research in Mathematics Education, 25*(1), 4–29.

Mason, J. (2000) "Asking Mathematical Questions Mathematically" *International Journal of Mathematical Education in Science and Technology, 31*(1), 97–111.

Mason, J., Burton, L., & Stacey, K. (2010) *Thinking Mathematically* (2nd ed.). Harlow, England: Prentice Hall.

McDougall, D. E. (2004) *School Mathematics Improvement Leadership Handbook.* Toronto, ON: Thomson Nelson.

Mcintosh, A., Reys, B., & Reys, R. (1992) "A Proposed Framework for Examining Basic Number Sense" *For the Learning of Mathematics, 12*(3), 2–44. Retrieved from http://www.jstor.org.myaccess.library.utoronto.ca/stable/40248053

McNeill, D. (2008) *Gesture and Thought.* Chicago, IL: University of Chicago Press.

Moss, J., & Bruce, C. D. (2016) *Taking Shape: Activities to Develop Geometric and Spatial Thinking. Grades K–2.* Don Mills, ON: Pearson Canada Inc.

National Council of Teachers of Mathematics (NCTM). (2014) *Principles and Standards for School Mathematics.* Reston, VA: NCTM.

National Council of Teachers of Mathematics (NCTM). (2000) *Principles to Actions: Ensuring Mathematical Success for All.* Reston, VA: NCTM.

National Research Council. (2001) *Adding It Up: Helping Children Learn Mathematics.* Washington, DC: National Academy Press.

Ontario Ministry of Education. (2013) *Learning for All: A Guide to Effective Assessment and Instruction for all Students, Kindergarten to Grade 12.* Toronto: Author. Retrieved from http://www.edu.gov.on.ca/eng/general/elemsec/speced/learningforall2013.pdf

Ontario Ministry of Education, Curriculum and Assessment Policy Branch. (2012) *Adolescent Literacy Guide – A Professional Learning Resource for Literacy, Grades 7–12.* Toronto, ON: Queen's Printer for Ontario.

Pólya, G. (1945) *How to Solve it: A New Aspect of Mathematical Method.* Princeton, N.J: Princeton University Press.

Ramani, G., & Siegler, R. (2008) "Promoting Broad and Stable Improvements in Low Income Children's Numerical Knowledge Through Playing Number Board Games" *Child Development, 79*(2), 375–394.

Reys, B. (1994) "Promoting Number Sense in the Middle Grades" *Mathematics Teaching in the Middle School, 1*(2), 114–120. Retrieved from http://www.jstor.org.myaccess.library.utoronto.ca/stable/41183170

Ritchhart, R., Church, M., & Morrison, K. (2011) *Making Thinking Visible.* San Francisco, CA: Jossey-Blass.

Scriven, M., & Paul, R. (1987) *Defining Critical Thinking.* Foundation for Critical Thinking. Retrieved from http://www.criticalthinking.org/aboutCT/define_critical_thinking.cfm

Sherin, M., Jacobs, V., & Philip, R. (2011) "On Noticing Teachers Noticing" In M. G. Sherin, V. R. Jacobs, & R. A. Philipp (Eds.), *Mathematics Teacher Noticing: Seeing Through Teachers' Eyes.* New York, NY: Taylor and Francis.

Silver, E. A., & Kenney, P. A. (1995) "Sources of Assessment Information for Instructional Guidance in Mathematics" In T.A. Romberg (Ed.), *Reform in School Mathematics and Authentic Assessment* (pp. 38–68). Albany, NY: State University of New York Press.

Simon, M., & Tzur, R. (2004) "Explicating the Role of Mathematical Tasks in Conceptual Learning: An Elaboration of the Hypothetical Learning Trajectory" *Mathematical Thinking and Learning, 6*(2), 91–104.

Small, M. (2005) *Professional Resources and Instruction for Mathematics Educators.* Toronto, ON: Nelson.

Small, M. (2005) *Number and Operations: Guide to Using the Developmental Map.* Toronto, ON: Thomson Nelson

Small, M. (2017) *Making Math Meaningful to Canadian Students, K–8.* Toronto, ON: Nelson Education Ltd.

Szilagyi, J., Clements, D. H., & Sarama, J. (2013) "Young Children's Understandings of Length Measurement: Evaluating a Learning Trajectory" *Journal for Research in Mathematics Education, 44*(3), 581–610.

Sztajn, P., Confrey, J., Wilson, P. H., & Edgington, C. (2012) "Learning Trajectory Based Instruction: Toward a Theory of Teaching" *Educational Researcher,* 41, 147–156.

Thames, M., & Ball, D. (2010) "What Math Knowledge Does Teaching Require?" *Teaching Children Mathematics, 17*(4), 220–229.

Thomas, K. (2006) "Students THINK: A Framework for Improving Problem Solving" *Teaching Children Mathematics, 13*(2), 86–95. Retrieved from http://www.jstor.org.myaccess.library.utoronto.ca/stable/41199843

Fosnot, C. (2014) *Models: Powerful Tools for Thinking.* Retrieved from https://thelearningexchange.ca/videos/models-powerful-tools-for-thinking/

Van de Walle, J., Karp, K., & Bay-Williams, J. M. (2017) *Elementary and Middle School Mathematics: Teaching Developmentally.* 9th Edition. New York, NY: Pearson.

Wiggins, G., & McTighe, J. (1998) *Understanding by Design.* Alexandria, VA: Association for Supervision and Curriculum Development.

Recommended Resources for Mathematics Professional Development

Beatty, R., & Bruce, C. (2012) *From Patterns to Algebra: Lessons for Exploring Linear Relationships.* Toronto, ON: Nelson Publications.

Boaler, J. (2015) *Mathematical Mindsets: Unleashing Students' Potential Through Creative Math, Inspiring Messages and Innovative Teaching.* San Francisco, CA: Wiley, Jossey-Bass.

Danielson, C. (2016) *Which One Doesn't Belong? A Shapes Book & Teacher's Guide.* Portland, ME: Stenhouse Publishers.

Danielson, C. (2018) *How Many? A Counting Book & Teacher's Guide.* Portsmouth, ME: Stenhouse Publishers.

Fiore, M., & Lebar, M. (2016) *Four Roles of the Numerate Learner.* Markham, ON: Pembroke Publishers.

Fiore, M., & Lebar, M. (2017) *Moving Math.* Markham, ON: Pembroke Publishers.

Franke, M. L., Kazemi, E., & Turrou, A. C. (2018) *Choral Counting & Counting Collections.* Portsmouth, NH: Stenhouse Publishers.

Hattie, J., Fisher, D., & Frey, N. (2017) *Visible Learning for Mathematics: What Works Best to Optimize Student Learning.* California: Corwin, A Sage Company.

Humphreys, C., & Parker, R. (2015) *Making Number Talks Matter: Developing Mathematical Practices and Deepening Understanding, Grades 4-10.* Portsmouth, ME: Stenhouse Publishers.

Humphreys, C., & Parker, R. (2018) *Digging Deeper: Making Number Talks Matter Even More.* Portsmouth, NH: Stenhouse Publishers.

Leland, C., Lewison, M., & Harste, J. (2012) *Teaching Children's Literature: It's Critical!* New York: Routledge.

Lewison, M., Leland, C., & Harste, J. C. (2015) *Creating Critical Classrooms: Reading and Writing with an Edge.* New York: Routledge.

Mason, J., Burton, L., & Stacey, K. (2010) *Thinking Mathematically* (2nd ed.). Harlow, England: Prentice Hall.

Moss, J., & Bruce, C. D. (2016) *Taking Shape: Activities to Develop Geometric and Spatial Thinking. Grades K–2.* Don Mills, ON: Pearson Canada Inc.

National Council of Teachers of Mathematics. (2014) *Principles to Actions: Ensuring Mathematical Success for All.* Reston, VA: NCTM.

Parrish, S. (2014) *Number Talks: Helping Children Build Mental Math and Computation Strategies.* Sausalito, CA: Math Solutions.

Ritchhart, R. (2015) *Creating Cultures of Thinking: The 8 Forces we must Master to Truly Transform our Schools.* San Francisco, CA: Wiley, Jossey-Bass.

Shumway, J. (2011) *Number Sense Routines K–3.* Portsmouth, ME: Stenhouse Publishers.

Shumway, J. (2018) *Number Sense Routines 3–5.* Portsmouth, ME: Stenhouse Publishers.

Small, M. (2005) *Professional Resources and Instruction for Mathematics Educators.* Toronto, ON: Nelson.

Small, M. (2005) *Number and Operations: Guide to Using the Developmental Map.* Toronto, ON: Thomson Nelson

Small, M. (2017) *Making Math Meaningful to Canadian Students, K–8.* Toronto, ON: Nelson Education Ltd.

Smith, M. S., & Stein, M. K. (2011) *5 Practices for Orchestrating Productive Mathematics Discussions.* Reston, VA: NCTM.

Van de Walle, J., Karp, K., & Bay-Williams, J. M. (2017) *Elementary and Middle School Mathematics: Teaching Developmentally.* 9th Edition. New York, NY: Pearson.

Vasquez, V. M. (2004) *Negotiating Critical Literacies with Young Children.* New York: Routledge.

Vasquez, V. M., & Felderman, C. B. (2012) *Technology and Critical Literacy in Early Childhood.* New York: Routledge.

Zager, T. J. (2017) *Becoming the Math Teacher You Wish You'd Had.* Portsmouth, ME: Stenhouse Publishers.

Index